To Ora

May the Lord
given Words message
your heart as you
need daily.
Blessings

[signature]

MW01244535

It's OK to be Beautiful!

Thirty Days to Healing, Health and Hope for a Beautiful Life

LORI A POTTS

itsoktobebeautiful.com

WESTBOW
PRESS®
A DIVISION OF THOMAS NELSON
& ZONDERVAN

WestBow Press books may be ordered through booksellers or by contacting:

WestBow Press
A Division of Thomas Nelson & Zondervan
1663 Liberty Drive
Bloomington, IN 47403
www.westbowpress.com
844-714-3454

ISBN: 978-1-6642-3348-5 (sc)
ISBN: 978-1-6642-3347-8 (hc)
ISBN: 978-1-6642-3349-2 (e)

Library of Congress Control Number: 2021909250

Print information available on the last page.

WestBow Press rev. date: 06/14/2021

This book is dedicated to my beautiful daughter, Korina and to all my heart-mothers, sisters and daughters. Then, now and yet to come.

Please note the thoughts and ideas expressed in this transcripts are based entirely on personal experience and opinion and are not intended to treat... of any kind. Always consult a licensed and accredited physician before incorporating supplements or herbs to your daily intake.

Forward

My name is Sarah Neal and I am a follower of Jesus Christ, wife to a rodeo Cowboy, mother to three children and a business executive within the beauty industry. I've known Lori since my early twenties. She and I met during one of the most trying seasons of my spiritual journey. I always thought of her as "the cool mom." She was stylish and fun and had a gift for connecting with women of all ages. Lori was the very first person in my life to break a "label" that had entrapped my heart since childhood.

If you've ever been "labeled," then you know exactly what I mean. A label usually comes in the form of a word or a phrase that is repeatedly spoken over you by strangers and those who know you addressing what they see or perceive about you. For me, that label was "beautiful." I'm sure you're thinking, "Oh my, you poor thing. How tragic and unfair." (Insert sarcasm) But here's the problem: A label, no matter how it sounds to the one doing the labeling, lands on the inside of a person (especially a child) and begins to take root as an identity. The more it is repeated, the more that seed is nourished and its roots begin to grow deep. Over time, your identity becomes rooted in that "thing" whatever it may be and clouds your true identity as a child of God. And wherever your identity is found, there also is the measure of your worth. Translation: If I am beautiful, pretty and attractive my life has meaning. If I am not, I'm of value to no one. I don't have to explain how obviously destructive this self-perception became as it tortured my heart and mind for decades. The cycle of sexual abuse throughout my childhood served only to reinforce this lie.

Then along came Lori. When the damage from this lie was at its all-time high, from an erratic eating disorder to toxic relationships and depression, she walked over to me at church one day and whispered one simple phrase: "Sarah, it's okay to be beautiful." My insides crumbled. I felt like I had been punched in the gut and set free all at the same time. She later gave me a bracelet inscribed with my new truth to remind me daily. The process of undoing a lie and embracing God's truth began to unfold in my life. Lori's words marked the beginning of my healing and I believe they can do the same for you.

I'm excited for you to journey with her over these next 30 days through the life-giving Word of God guided by the Holy Spirit.

I pray you internalize ever truth and take captive every lie. I pray you encounter the pure and relentless love of your Heavenly Father. As He peruses your heart, May He find it and heal it in Jesus' name.

Preface

I was twelve years old and my daddy had just picked me up from school. I was an awkward girl at that age, freckles and a few pre-adolescent blemishes adorning my complexion. I was twenty pounds overweight, and had stringy straight mousy, dirty-blond hair, cut in an attempt of feathered bangs. Oh that winged hair-do that all girls had in 1983, with Farrah Faucet and Charlies Angels setting the trend at the time. We were in his truck on our way home as we passed a pack of popular girls walking down the side of the road. Each one was dressed in the latest fashionable jeans and logo tees; those perfect feathered bangs and not forbidden to wear makeup. This gang of friends always looked a few years older than most girls in my class. I felt the heart wrenching pain of inadequacy in their presence and even more so now in daddy's truck, watching them giggle and dance together as they made their way down the road. I was completely engulfed in my cluttered, self-condemning thoughts as my dad turns to me and said "why can't you be as cute as those girls, huh? Are they in your class?" "Yes daddy, they are." I answered. He didn't say anything else on the way home, but just those two, earth shattering sentences, uttered out of my father's mouth, is all it took to write those lies on my heart. "My own dad thinks I'm ugly!" "He would rather have one of those girls for his daughter." "I will never be good enough to please my dad or anyone else."

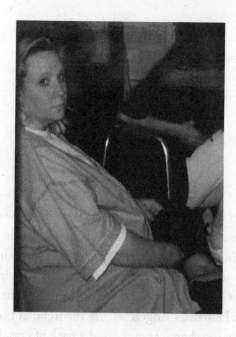

What could have prevented me from ingesting the pain from those words in my heart? What could have prevented a weight gain up to 270 pounds and spiral in to self-destruction? Something I didn't know at the time, but God has revealed in my life lessons after lessons. Through reading about a few of those lessons, I pray you experience the grace of skipping past potential wounds and hurts; I pray your life journey may be a joy filled travel of health, wellness and peace. You see, if the heartache and pain I have walked through is all for this moment, writing to you precious child, it was all for His purpose. It was all for your chance to gain knowledge to identify, overcome and have victory through the healing power of our Father, God.

ALL things work together for His good, for His purpose, for His plan He has for each of us. This is how deep His love is for us, this is the passion He has for each one of us, individually. In the scripture to follow, David never mentions once his outward appearance but emphasis is placed exclusively on the inward parts, "his soul knows it well." Not his thighs or belly … not his weight, height or the shape of his nose, but his inward parts; the parts you can't see. Transformation begins in the heart, through salvation in receiving Jesus Christ as our Lord and Savior. Transformation progresses to our soul through the renewing of our minds. The outward, physical appearance is superficial, it's only skin deep.

God created each one of us in His image and leaves nothing undone. Everything He does is complete. When we look in our mirrors and we are unhappy with what we see, we are saying "God, you missed something!" We are saying, "God, you made a mistake!" Is that possible? Surely not!

Does the clay have the right to call out the potter? Would we dare tell the artist his painting is flawed?

We are not seeing our person as a whole, we are seeing the outward appearance only, and that's just a third of our total being! What we can't physically see is our spirit man and our soul. These are the two parts of the three combined sum of our being. The outward, physical beauty comes from the transformation of our heart and mind, illuminating from the inside, out. This is where the healing begins. This is where true beauty starts.

"FOR YOU FORMED MY INWARD PARTS;
YOU KNITTED ME TOGETHER IN MY MOTHER'S WOMB.
I PRAISE YOU, FOR I AM FEARFULLY
AND WONDERFULLY MADE.
WONDERFUL ARE YOUR WORKS,
MY SOUL KNOWS IT VERY WELL."
PSALMS 139:13-14 ESV

Introduction

Going back to the beginning.

Have you ever heard someone say, "Man, if I could just go back and do that again I would do it all so different?"

We get down in the rewind, replay part of our brains and we get lost in there trying to figure out how we got where we are right now. Stuck in the day in and day out, we set those pondering thoughts aside, we push them down deep in our gut and let them go, just to push forward in life.

Consider when we get lost and we're driving, driving, driving and don't know exactly where we're going, we just have an address to our destination. We take a wrong turn and all of a sudden, we wind up on some long dirt road that leads to the scariest shack-backwards piece of property. Now we are left with visions of Michael Myers running towards our car from behind the scavenged remains of some random house we are now sitting in front of.

The only thought going through our mind is how did we get here?

The quickest way to get un-lost, is to go back where we started, turn around and move back down that same road. Go backwards until we get to the wrong turn we took.

Imagine if we go back to the beginning, not yesterday not last week or last month or even to the beginning of our lifetime. But what if we go back to the very furthest beginning of everything. The beginning of time, when God spoke this world into creation, the true beginning.

Over the next thirty days we are going to explore the process of creation. Each of the six days of creation, God manifested a new subject, a new matter, a new need for survival in this world. Let's go back to the very beginning and break down our very need for light, the need for water, the need for ferment, the need for trees and vegetation, animals that roam, and last but not least, that yearning need and desire for relationship with each other. As humans, He gave us dominion over this big, beautiful world for our benefit as His lavish gift. So let us explore, let us go back to the very beginning to find these gifts we lost and now find ourselves missing from our lives today.

Each day, for the next thirty days we will begin with focus on the day specific creational element, a scriptural promise with a life experience insight to realistically apply it to our every-day, day in and day out. A daily mirror message for us straight from the creator himself. We will learn a physical activity to stimulate wellness, and healthy eating tid-bits, each designed to easily be incorporated in our daily routines and diet. Take notes along the way because you will want to circle back around and re-read your thoughts to monitor your progression.

Ideally, all of the daily content combined will require a devotion of fifteen to twenty minutes. Considering it only takes twenty one days to acquire a habit, thirty days will lay the foundation for healing, heath, wellness and revelation of just how precious each of us are in this world, just how each of us are specifically woven in to this intricate tapestry of life, and darling, how this world is so much the better place with each one of us in it!

Mirror Message of the Day

When we consider what beauty--true beauty is, the old saying "beauty is in the eye of the beholder" comes to mind. In Ecclesiastes 3:11 ESV it says "He has made everything beautiful in its time. Also, he has put eternity into man's heart, yet so that he cannot find out what God has done from the beginning to the end." The archetype of beauty is not as the world would portray in social media, magazine covers and in Hollywood. Nor should it be relational to our outward appearance, but from the inside, our deepest inward parts springing out. Be mindful not to define yourself by the opinion of others, life experience or temporal emotions. Know you have been defined the moment you came under the blood of Jesus Christ, and you have been defined by your Creator and Father God. You are defined as fearfully and wonderfully made, you are His righteousness, and you are His precious child.

GOD'S PROMISE REMAINS: PHILIPPIANS 1:6 ESV
"AND I AM SURE OF THIS, THAT HE WHO BEGAN
A GOOD WORK IN YOU WILL BRING IT TO
COMPLETION AT THE DAY OF JESUS CHRIST."

Day 1

Light is so good! It brings comfort in the dark of night, establishing a peace in the evidence that no dangers are lurking under the bed, or behind a door. Its' calm is indescribable, incomparable and irreplaceable.

1 John 1:5 ESV says, "God is light and there is no darkness in Him at all." It's no surprise this was God's starting point in creation, the epitome of God himself made evident in the formless and empty void that was nothing. God spoke it out, and it was so, and has given us that same power. We speak forth light into the darkness when we tell the cashier at

the store, she has the most beautiful eyes! We speak forth light when we tell our spouse, our children, our parents, friends, our God "I love you." We speak forth light when we stand in the mirror this morning, and say directly to the reflection there, "you are loved, you are valued, and you are the beloved child of the one true King! Salvation through Jesus Christ has clothed you in righteousness that no darkness can possibly blot you out. You see sweetheart, once you're His, darkness can never extinguish the light. -John 1:5

Wellness

Vitamin D, the source of life in this human body and ninety five percent of the human population acquires their daily intake by incidental sunlight exposure. However, Vitamin D deficiency is at epidemic proportions! It's wild to think that just ten minutes in direct sunlight a day provides 10,000 units of vitamin D to your body, and will aid in the prevention of bone density loss, cancer, diabetes, autoimmune disorders, hormone imbalances and more. Go outside today, get some sunshine in your life. If weather or a health condition prevents outdoor exposure, sitting in an open, sunlit window will work too.

Healthy

Fruit has received a pretty bad name for itself lately but you see, I'm a firm believer that for everything God has given us to enjoy, the enemy creates a smooth imposter to destroy! The white table sugar we all know and grew up loving, heaped high on our cereal is not even close to being derived from nature once commercially processed and will wreak havoc in our bodies. The sugar we digest by eating a whole, unadulterated piece of fruit is worlds apart! Just by eating one medium sized, organic (yes, it matters!) apple, you are detoxing your liver, boosting your immune system, feeding your good gut bacteria, strengthening your teeth and preventing a whole plethora of diseases. Apples are a little snuggle hug to your gut! Make it a point to have one today. Not sure which kind? My personal choice is honey crisp, second choice pink lady.

Mirror Message of the Day

I am a new creation! Everything old is gone forever and I am new.
1 Corinthians 5:17

Notes

_____

_____

_____

_____

_____

_____

_____

_____

_____

_____

_____

_____

Day 2

Google dictionary defines "good" as desired or approved and having the qualities required for a particular role. We reinforce positive behavior by speaking the word good, when training a pet, employee, even our children. Experiences, memories, thoughts and dreams can be good. We label foods, clothes, colors, cars and even people as good as if our standard seal of approval increases its value to the masses. Truth is, everyone has their own scale and valued sets of criteria to stamp the big word "good" on any given thing, person or circumstance. The real question here is, what God meant when He said "light was good". The origin is the word "tob" which means pleased, God was pleased with the light. He was pleased when Solomon asked for wisdom in governing His people in 1 Kings 3:10 NIV after that, God granted him all he asked for. God was also pleased with Jesus for his obedience in baptism at the hands of John the Baptist, Matthew 3:17. In these days of grace, pleasing God doesn't require any effort once you're clothed in the righteousness of Christ, but it's our faith God is pleased with. Faith pleases God more than anything else, plain and simple, we stand on it, live by it, breath it in and shout it out in our praises to Him. It comes in all sizes, but all that you need is the itty bitty, teeny tiny size of a mustard seed. By faith, we understand the universe was created by the spoken word of God, not from things visible. We all have our moments of doubt, and mine came when a dear friend's nine year old son was battling inoperable brain cancer. The night he passed on to heaven, I was angry at God, questioning, throwing doubts and laying down my faith in a grand fashion. Sobbing ugly tears, I sat there in full self-pity swing of things, when my husband asked why I was crying. I explained, how could a God that loves us so much not answer this plea for healing, I didn't understand and was physically, mentally and spiritually broken. He told me to look at him and then spoke five words that brought me to my knees; "It's none of your business", and he was right. I am certain, God was pleased with his answer that night, as it grew my faith by trusting in a loving God that always works all things, even the painful, heart-ripping things together for our good.

Wellness

Did you know light contains color tones and impacts our moods throughout the day? It's true! Light can be either warm or cool, depending on the Kelvin temperature. It's just the reverse of what typically we think when considering temperature, because it has nothing to do with hot or cold. The higher the Kelvin temperature, the cooler the light, the lower the kelvin temperature, the warmer the light! Commercial buildings are flooded with cool temperature lighting to stimulate productivity and keep us more alert and focused. At home, it's best to use warm hued bulbs to encourage a more comforting relaxed environment, and set our minds to a more calm and peaceful mood.

Healthy

Poly-what?? Polyphenols found in coffee, tea and yes, dark chocolate are an incredible, God given micronutrients and powerful antioxidant that is so beneficial to incorporate into your daily diet to combat all kinds of virus, bacteria and toxins floating around in our bodies. They are also found in a ton of fruits and vegetable sources, but most plentiful, at one hundred milligrams per serving, in the mentioned above. Not a coffee drinker? Okay! A cup of black pekoe or green tea will provide you with a generous portion. Add a teaspoon of raw, unfiltered local honey and that right there will be just a little cup of healthy heaven!

Mirror Message of the Day

I am dearly loved, holy and chosen by Father God.
Colossians 3:12

Notes

_____

_____

_____

_____

_____

_____

_____

_____

_____

_____

_____

_____

Day 3

"...Then He separated the light from the darkness.
Genesis 1:4 NLT

I watch a lot of HGTV and my favorite shows are the renovation series where they take this old run down, left for dead house and completely bring it back to life! Fresh coat of paint, move a few walls, add some cabinetry and voila! Beauty at its finest! I watch in awe as they work so diligently, always taking that house to a new level, without complaints of aches in their bodies or a contractor that didn't show, or even that pipe that sprung a leak at the most in-opportune time. Nope, they just act like it's another day and just part of the process, cutting up, laughing and moving on to another layer towards the excellence that is to come. Towards the end of the show, they bring the owners-to-be to their made-over home for the reveal, and it's always the best part! They ooh and awe and get so giddy over the little details in each completely revived room! The excitement is contagious as the creators share their story of how each room came together perfectly, through the challenges, the setbacks, the trials and hardships and how delighted they are that through it all, the end result was so worth it.

I have always said, houses are like people, they are living, breathing structures and just need love and attention to light them up! Well, I feel like we start out like that rickety shack of a house, all dark and dingy inside, but once Jesus shows up on the scene, His radiant light shines through us, stripping back the layers of bitterness, rage, anger, harsh words and ugliness like those renovators do those houses. Philippians 2:14 says to do all things without grumbling or disputing, so that we may shine as lights in the world.

We can complain when tests and trials come, or we can choose to trust that when the layers are pulled back, what will be revealed works out to be even better than we could ever imagine! I think shining our light in the world is like those designers showing off their work to the new owners. It's finding someone walking through a similar life circumstance, a layer yet to be pulled back and reaching out to say, "I understand, and let me share my story of how Jesus brought me through to the other sun shiny side of it."

Wellness

Every living, breathing person has a circadian rhythm that regulates our wake and sleep patterns. There are life factors that contribute to the schedules our bodies follow such as diet, exercise, alarm clocks! The most influencing factor may be the amount of sunlight we are exposed to on a daily basis. Darkness tells our brains it's time to sleep and light tells our brains it's time to wake! The artificial light, "bad light" we expose ourselves to after dark can throw this rhythm out of whack and wreak havoc on our health if we become sleep deprived. To ensure you're limiting the amount of "bad light" you're exposing yourself to, there are a few easy applications to apply to your home and electronic devices that can help. To decrease the amount of tossy turny sleepless bed time and increase your amount of awe-inspiring, restful sleep, use blue blocker glasses or adjust the settings on TV's, phones, tablets to warm tone. Most offer a night setting in the display menu.

Healthy

"When life gives you lemons …" Every morning when I wake up, I begin the day with half an organic lemon squeezed into twenty four ounces of filtered water, and wait thirty minutes before eating or drinking anything else. While sleeping, our liver is hard at work filtering and cleansing the mud and muck we expose our bodies to through diet and environmental toxins. The nutritional properties found in lemon, combined with clean, filtered water flood through your digestive system to wake up those vital organs and flush out the nasty waste your liver has worked so very hard to save you from. Don't be alarmed if you feel nauseous, it's actually a good thing!

Mirror Message of the Day

I am protected, healed and whole safe under the wings of my Father God. Psalms 91:3-4

_____

_____

_____

_____

_____

_____

_____

_____

_____

_____

_____

_____

Day 4

"God called the light "day" and
the darkness "night" ...
Genesis 1:5 NLT

As far back as I can remember, I slept snuggled between my mom and dad, until that fateful day of my baby sister's homecoming. I was seven years old and my world stopped turning the moment we picked her and mom up from the hospital, or so it seemed to me at the time. It was Christmas Eve and everyone kept going on and on about how Robin was everyone's best Christmas gift ever! Yeah right! Even though we had a crib for her, that very same night she displaced me forever from the safe haven, warm cozy, cuddled up close in daddy's back place in their king sized nest! This did not come close to fitting my seven year old brain's criteria of best present ever, and embarked within me a very real struggle with insecurity and fear. Fear is the number one weapon Satan uses against us, and has been since Adam and Eve fell in to sin. Genesis 3:10. From there, the battle was on! Abraham was afraid, which caused him to lie about the identity of Sarah, Moses was afraid and kept the Israelites roaming the desert for forty years, Jonah was afraid and ended up in the belly of a whale, the accounts go on and on and on! I was afraid, when the lights went out at night. It was the gut wrenching, heart stopping, can't breathe, move or scream kind of fear that washed over my little body and had no mercy. I am certain now I must have driven my family insane from lack of sleep most nights. My life verse is "The Lord is my light and my salvation; whom shall I fear? The Lord is the strength of my life; of whom shall I be afraid." Psalms 27:1 KJV and I would recite it out loud, over and over until I'd fall asleep and occasionally still do to this day. There's power in the spoken word of God and the only way to combat fear and triumph over the enemy is to shine a little light on it.

Wellness

The healing power of light is quickly becoming a center stage treatment for such an array of conditions. Laser Light Therapy is being used to eliminate cancer, relieve neuropathy pain, stimulate bone regeneration, reverse hair loss, unwrinkled skin, fight aging and even eradicate toenail fungus! As the use of light becomes more prevalent, I would hope insurance companies will recognize it as a viable treatment and begin to cover the costs. Infrared light therapy offers similar pain reducing benefits and can even speed healing from viruses and infections in the body. When I first discovered infrared, I immediately went on the search for a home spa, and was able to score a nice, used one for a fraction of the cost. A lot of health and fitness chains also offer the use of infrared light beds included with their membership.

Healthy

What's green, bumpy and shaped like an egg? An avocado of course! Consuming one whole avocado a day is high on my priority list, seriously … one daily. They are rich, creamy and so yummy spread across a toasted piece of sprouted grain bread, diced up in a salad, mixed with salsa for a great guacamole or if you are not a fan of the taste, make it disappear by blending it in your favorite smoothie. What will happen when you consume one on the daily, you ask? Gorgeous skin, energy galore, increase brain power, improve heart health, sharpen vision, lower A1C levels and actually end up feeling fuller, longer after eating so you don't eat as much. That beautiful, tasty green goo has me captured with the dramatic changes I've seen in my health and I definitely feel the difference if I skip it!

Mirror Message of the Day

I am strengthened through Christ and can do all the things!
Philippians 4:13

Notes

Day 5

"...AND EVENING PASSED AND MORNING
CAME, MARKING THE FIRST DAY."
GENESIS 1:5 NLT

"Time, time, time ... see what's become of me."

This is the opening line to a song made popular in the Eighty's by a group called The Bangles, describing the seasons of change, how things go from the hazy shade of winter to the hope of spring. It was a catchy little tune and was quickly one of my favorites back in the day. But better yet, I love the way Ecclesiastes 3:1 AMP describes seasons; "there is a season (a time appointed) for everything and a time for every delight and event or purpose under heaven." God's purpose for seasons is a larger part of the umpteen billion processes in place, day and night. Life is constantly in motion, everything coming, going, changing, growing, turning over, falling apart and then together put back in place. Each morning, every day we start with God's renewed mercies and we are off and running that dizzy race again! No matter what each day holds, His grace is always sufficient and allots just the exact amount we need to maneuver this wild life's highway and when we trust Him with all the details, things always work for our greatest benefit. Each day is a gift, and filled with excellent opportunities for us to shine love on each other. At the end of the day, it's not about the fanatical events that make us question our sanity, it's all about that little light shining through us by helping that lady load her groceries in the car, or the smile you gave to the baby peeking at you over her momma's shoulder, paying for the man's coffee behind you in line or simply greeting your spouse with an excitable hug and kiss.. Those glimpses of kindness, shared between us in the midst of the chaos are I believe, the good, and perfect gifts of each day and everything the Father desires for us. James 1:17 AMP says "Every good thing given and every perfect gift is from above; it comes down from the Father of lights [the Creator and Sustainer of the heavens], in whom there is no variation [no rising or setting] or shadow cast by His turning [for He is perfect and never changes]. In this ever changing world, it's everything to know God is the perfect calm and constant foundation we can rest in. Make the very most of your gift today, carefully considering what thread you will weave into your tapestry of time.

Wellness

The energy from the sun produces 6,000 times the energy in one day than could be consumed by the entire world's population in one year! Wow! That's a lot of power! It's currently the least expensive, cleanest, and readily available source of energy. So, why aren't we harnessing and using this energy everywhere? Good question! Unfortunately, converting the sun's energy into usable energy is quite costly, and no sustainable method of storage exists for this energy during periods of night or limited sunlight. Until technology expands, there are solar panels to supplement energy usage for our homes and even portable phone chargers that are solar powered available on amazon.

Healthy

Cha-cha-cha-chia!! Chia seeds are a super food that has become a staple in my diet, and is a daily must have! Those tiny little powerhouses pack a huge punch of antioxidants, minerals, omega 3s, ALAs, protein, and thirty seven percent of your daily fiber in just one tablespoon. They are one of the best defenses against aging skin, free radical damage and preventing oxidative stress. Just by adding these seeds you are preventing bone loss, cancer, high blood pressure, digestive disorders, and more! They have a texture similar to tapioca when expanded and practically no taste, so they are a perfect addition to unflavored yogurt with fruit or your delicious, nutritious morning smoothie we will have you drinking by completion of this book!

Mirror Message of the Day

I am more than a conqueror through Jesus who loves me.
Romans 8:37

Notes

_____

_____

_____

_____

_____

_____

_____

_____

_____

_____

_____

_____

Day 6

AND GOD SAID, "LET THERE BE AN EXPANSE
IN THE MIDST OF THE WATERS, AND LET IT
SEPARATE THE WATERS FROM THE WATERS."
GENESIS 1:6 ESV

Have you ever been hit so hard in the stomach or fell flat on your back and had the wind knocked out of you? It's such a scary moment, not to be able to do the one thing that literally keeps us alive! I remember it happening to me for the first time, I came up screaming blood curdling screams running inside the house, crying the ugliest big tears you ever saw and told my mom I almost died! She gave me a hug and a kiss on the head and reassured me I was going to be just fine and had a long life ahead of me. I believed her, and sure enough, I'm still here, alive and breathing! My child's heart and mind believed her without one ounce of doubt, I believed her because she's my mom and I believed her because of the relationship we shared. You see, whenever I would fall down, she was there to brush me off, set me on my feet and kiss my head and make it better, building that trust, one day at a time, over a lifetime. Our relationship with God is built the same way, as a child of God, when life comes along and knocks us down, we cry out to Him, lift praises to Him, thanking Him, because you trust in God that no matter what knocked the wind out of you, He's going to bring you through to the other side of the pain. Standing firm on the promises He made us in His word, we believe, trust and hold strong and once we are back upright and breathing, we are forever changed, our story grows, our faith grows and the next time that sucker punch to the gut comes along, we see it for what it is and it doesn't knock us to our knees. Psalms 46:1 ESV "God is our refuge and strength, a very present help in trouble", Psalms 91:15 ESV

"When he calls me, I will answer him I will be with him in trouble; I will rescue him and honor him." 1 Peter 5:7 ESV "cast all your anxieties on him, because he cares for you."

Wellness

The air we breathe, have you ever considered it and how perfectly perfect the percentages in the composition are for sustaining life as we know it? Oxygen in the air contributes a vital role in the production of energy synthesis in our bodies, that is why when we rest our breathing slows, and if we are working out or active our rate of breaths per minute increases. I have found it so helpful, when that three o'clock in the afternoon slowsy doseys hit, if I take ten deep, purposeful breaths, I can increase my energy almost immediately! As an added bonus, if you will incorporate this activity several times during the day, by increasing oxygen in your blood, you increase cellular function and promote the continued healing processes your body is constantly carrying out.

Healthy

Cuckoo for coconut water! Coconut water is a perfect gift of hydration, and beneficial in so many ways. When I am super busy at work and not able to get my water in, I head straight to my coconut water for relief and instant refreshment as soon as I can. It's an excellent source of potassium, along with other minerals and so much more effective than overly sweetened sports drinks or electrolyte drinks when recovering from dehydration. Coconut water aids in digestion and acts as an anti-parasitic, antiviral, antibacterial agent in your intestinal tract and definitely on my list of daily must-haves. When selecting a brand, read the ingredients, you want to make sure you are getting the real deal, not concentrate, and additives along with your coconut water. My first choice is Sprouts brand 100 percent coconut water NOT from concentrate.

Mirror Message of the Day

I am Father God's masterpiece creation! I am made new in Christ Jesus to do all the things He has planned for me.
Ephesians 2:10

Notes

_____

_____

_____

_____

_____

_____

_____

_____

_____

_____

_____

_____

_____

Day 7

"AND GOD MADE THE EXPANSE AND SEPARATED THE
WATERS THAT WERE UNDER THE EXPANSE FROM THE WATERS
THAT WERE ABOVE THE EXPANSE. AND IT WAS SO."
GENESIS 1:7 ESV

People are usually surprised when I tell them I started smoking when I was twenty nine years old. I heard it would help me lose weight and reduce stress. The peer pressure at the college I attended part time and from my older sister didn't help in discouraging me. There seemed to be so much fun and activities going on during those smoke breaks and who wants to be left out of that! The deepest, juiciest gossip is exchanged during those moments and you're instantly part of the cool clique, or so it seems. I held on to that habit until three years ago, at the age of forty seven, when God started gently urging me to tear that layer off of my life. When God called me to lay it down was the moment it became disobedience for me and became a priority to start laying the foundation to change once and for all. Hiding it from my church family was easy, I would shower and dress for church the morning before service so I would be free from the stink of it, but attending special events in the evening was out of question in fear of being found out. The funny thing is, non-smokers can smell it anyway. When you smoke, it's on your clothes, in your hair, steals your breath and permeates your very skin layers. You can't smell it yourself, because you are right smack dab in the midst of it. You see, no one wants others to see our disobedience when we walk outside the authority of God. Sin separates us. It's ugly, disgusting, embarrassing and hinders us from moving forward in our spiritual growth and relationship with Jesus. Did God love me any less? Of course not! That's not even possible, you see God sees us blameless and clothed in righteousness, through the power of the redemptive blood of Jesus. Philippians 1:6 ESV says "And I am sure of this, that he who began a good work in you will bring it to completion at the day of Jesus Christ." I am so thankful He didn't leave me in my mess, I am so thankful I took that step forward in faith and I'm so thankful when standing in front of what I thought was an unmovable wall of glass, was not glass at all! It was a thin, flimsy sheet of plastic wrap, and easily broke away with that one simple act of obedience, stepping straight into the freedom on the other side.

Wellness

Did you know that the first twelve hours of your last cigarette, your blood oxygen levels return to normal and all excess carbon monoxide is removed from your body? At twenty four hours, the risk for a stroke, high blood pressure and cardiovascular events are already starting to decrease. In two days the nerve endings for the senses of taste and smell start healing and be heightened. Within three short days, all nicotine will be out of your bloodstream and you are steady on the road to healing! Keep going, as one month after your last cigarette, your lung capacity increases to take in and use oxygen more efficiently in your body, increasing your physical endurance. You are no longer a slave to the chemically driven craving the tobacco companies work so hard to flood your brain with.

Healthy

Oh, the wonderful healing power of ginger! Ginger has been used in naturopathic medicine for over 2,500 years and is especially beneficial to those suffering with COPD caused from cigarette smoking. Ginger reduces inflammation and in trial studies increases oxygen levels after consuming the spice. I like to add one fourth of a teaspoon of organic ground ginger to a few of my favorite morning shakes, but can creatively be added to your diet. It's a favorite among expecting moms, as it curbs morning sickness or nausea and helps with digestion. Among other benefits, it improves heart health, reduces cancer risk and naturally boost your immune system.

Mirror Message of the Day

I am provided for and Father God supplies all my needs according to the riches of His glory in Christ Jesus.
Philippians 4:19

Notes

_____

_____

_____

_____

_____

_____

_____

_____

_____

_____

_____

_____

Day 8

"And God called the expanse heaven. And there was evening and there was morning, the second day."
Genesis 1:8 ESV

Heaven ... growing up in church, I would listen to the preacher explain what it will be like and would daydream about the indescribable beauty that would eventually be our home at the end of our lifetime. Streets of gold, lined with emeralds, rubies and diamonds filled my young mind with wonder of how it would all be designed. Pastor would talk about the mansions in heaven and with my dad a contractor, I would imagine Jesus in his white coveralls, leather tan tool belt and pencil stuck behind His ear building us all little mansions along those gold streets. John 14:2 describes to us how Jesus is preparing our place, so it must be true! My passion for houses began young, as I was Momma's little helper before I started school and would travel with her, job to job, running errands. I would explore the nooks and crannies of the multitude of homes my dad worked on, and was always so eager to help my dad do any little thing he would allow me to do. I was always so proud to perform my made-up, keep me busy and occupied "jobs" for him and daddy would lift me up in his arms, giving me a kiss on the cheek for all my hard work!

In the Word, we read that that Jesus came down to be about the will of His Father in John 6:38 and as His children, we desire to do His daily work, bringing heaven down to earth and extending the Father's love to those we encounter daily. It can be people we work with, friends, acquaintances we see at local businesses but most importantly our family, for our spouse and children need our love and kindness more. They need to feel the acceptance, unconditional compassion and understanding when we are in our most raw moments, genuine, agape love from our Father in Heaven. It teaches, instructs and speaks volumes of the authenticity of our daily walk with Jesus, and will carry through to generations to come.

Wellness

The second day. Have you ever wondered why day two after a workout always hurts the worst? It's called delayed onset muscle soreness or DOMS. That discomfort you feel is damage to your muscle fibers that are reached during strenuous workouts or weight training, not typically used on a daily basis. The soreness you experience is perfectly normal and will recover and resolve itself, typically by day three.

Healthy

There is something so soothing and calming about drinking a warm fresh brewed cup of tea! The medicinal use of teas has been around since the second century BC and with good reason, considering the vast array of healing properties found in the multitude of herbs, flowers and plants. One of my favorites is green tea combined with ginger root and hibiscus, yum! I always use filtered water and organic teas from Traditional Medicinal.

Mirror Message of the Day

I am free and set apart from the law not to ever be a slave, because Christ Jesus has truly set me free!
Galatians 5:1

_____

_____

_____

_____

_____

_____

_____

_____

_____

_____

_____

_____

_____

_____

Day 9

"AND GOD SAID, "LET THE WATERS UNDER THE
HEAVENS BE GATHERED TOGETHER INTO ONE PLACE,
AND LET THE DRY LAND APPEAR." AND IT WAS SO."
GENESIS 1:9 ESV

At the rear of our property we have a creek that runs through the border. Its picturesque beauty is quiet and peaceful, and over the years has served as the backdrop for many a photo or two. At the very edge, you have to be careful not to get too close where the water has resided because you will sink down in the mere and wreak havoc pulling your foot out, usually without a shoe attached!

When God parted the Jordan for Joshua, can you imagine how mired the bottom of the river should have been? Yet, the account read in Joshua 3:17 describes they stood firmly on dry ground until all the nation of Israel had passed over. What a miraculous wonder it must have been to be standing in the middle of the Jordan river, the twelve priests carrying the Ark of the Covenant at its estimated weight of 600 plus pounds … can you imagine the probable sinkage on that? But God had other plans, He had plans to show the Israelites the fulfillment of His promise, to deliver them from their enemies and establish their place in the land. He showed the same promise to Moses at the Red Sea, and then again for Joshua as documented in Joshua 4:22-24 ESV "then you shall let your children know, 'Israel passed over this Jordan on *dry ground*.' For the LORD your God dried up the waters of the Jordan for you until you passed over, as the LORD your God did to the Red Sea, which he dried up for us until we passed over, so that all the peoples of the earth may know that the hand of the LORD is mighty, that you may fear the LORD your God forever."

That same God that showed Himself out to the Israelites is the same God we serve today, and craves to show out for you and me in that same miraculous way. Luke 18:27 ESV says "What is impossible with man is possible with God." Hebrews 2:4 ESV "He bore signs and wonders and various miracles and by gifts of the Holy Spirit." Jesus himself explains to the disciples that all the miracles they had seen, could not compare to what was to come through the gift of the Holy Spirit. (John 14:12) What miracle are you believing God for today? I assure you darling, in a wink of an eye, He can and will, then in the same accord, we will say to our children and our children's children "look what God has done".

Wellness

Have you ever ditched your shoes and walked barefoot on the shore of a lake on the beach? I always feel like I'm completely re-energized just from these brief moments of serenity and feeling the earth beneath my feet. There's actual science to back up that euphoric experience and explains the why behind it. Our bodies run on electrical current. As the *Journal of Environmental and Public Health* states:

[It is an established, though not widely appreciated fact, that the Earth's surface possesses a limitless and continuously renewed supply of free or mobile electrons. The Earth's negative charges can create a stable internal bioelectrical environment for the normal functioning of all body systems which may be important for setting the biological clock, regulating circadian rhythms and balancing cortisol levels.] Go ahead, kick off those shoes and run barefoot in the grass!

Healthy

What is smooth, rich, dark, creamy and absolutely delicious? Chocolate! Choosing to be healthy doesn't mean you have to leave this decadent behind because cocoa is one of the most mineral and antioxidant rich foods you can eat. The bad comes from what manufacturers or you are pairing with the chocolate. There are some great brands out there like Lily's chocolate that make great once in a while treats that will delight your soul and not bankrupt your get healthy efforts. My favorite is to add a packet of Cocoa Via chocolate to my morning shake once a week. Cocoa contains naturally occurring metals that if consumed too often, can build up in your body, so I always recommend limiting consumption to once or twice a week.

Mirror Message of the Day

I am loved with an everlasting love by my Father in heaven.
Jeremiah 31:3

Notes

_____

_____

_____

_____

_____

_____

_____

_____

_____

_____

_____

_____

Day 10

"GOD CALLED THE DRY LAND EARTH, AND
THE WATERS THAT WERE GATHERED SEAS.
AND GOD SAW THAT IT WAS GOOD."
GENESIS 1:10 ESV

Occasional separation from the noise of our lives is necessary for personal growth. When our babies are little it's a momma's safe haven escape just to go to the bathroom alone! I have a time set aside in the morning to read the word, listen to worship music and pray. This time is first on my agenda, after my lemon water. This time has become so special for me just to draw near to Father God, cast my cares for the day and letting the sweet Holy Spirit wash over me. Many are those mornings I don't "feel" God's presence, I don't get that washed over experience or divine insight, or word. What happens when we don't get the warm cozy fuzzy's? I praise Him anyway, I thank Him anyway, because in faith He wants me to continue, knowing He's there no matter what I "feel". His word promises He will never leave us or forsake us. (Hebrews 13:5). Consider it a test to increase our steadfastness, according to James 1:3. When you are talking to someone on the phone and the conversation turns silent, do you question whether they are still there, still connected? Well no we don't and it's the same way with God. He is still there, still connected. You see, feelings will sell you out every time, because they are fickle and unpredictable and can lead you into a world of mess. The enemy can create all kinds of drama up in your mind and get it running rampant with imaginations! Faith is not about a feeling, it's about trusting in the one true God, knowing He always has your best in store. I choose to keep growing, keep seeking His face, because I know when Father God does show out, He never, ever disappoints. "Love Never Fails!" 1 Corinthians 13:8 NIV

Wellness

Outdoor cross country walking is not only a great way to show your cardiovascular system some love, but the rough terrain is great for conditioning and strength training all in one! According to Nordic Academy, 90 percent of your musculoskeletal system engages, and 46 percent more calories are burned than regular track or street walking. It's also great for strengthening and stabilizing your core, encouraging better posture and stance. Not to mention you are outside, in the sunlight and fresh air and at the end of your walk you can kick your shoes off and get some of that grounding action we've talked about!

Healthy

Soil based probiotics are creating quite a noise for themselves in the health industry and I just want to say, I'm not convinced. I have a hard time stomaching the fact of voluntarily ingesting spores of bacteria that are actually undefined in my body. Something about this is just so wrong and so you heard it here. Years from now we will learn about the dangers of using this type of supplement, but in the meantime, I will continue to use what works for me, which is a generous portion of raw, organic sauerkraut! I am particularly fond of the brand Wild brine Dill and Garlic kraut. It is found in the refrigerated section at Sprouts or Whole Foods. So good!

Mirror Message of the Day

I am fully accepted and approved by my heavenly Father in Christ Jesus. John 6:37

Notes

_____

_____

_____

_____

_____

_____

_____

_____

_____

_____

_____

_____

_____

_____

Day 11

AND GOD SAID, "LET THE EARTH SPROUT VEGETATION,
PLANTS YIELDING SEED, AND FRUIT TREES BEARING
FRUIT IN WHICH IS THEIR SEED, EACH ACCORDING
TO ITS KIND, ON THE EARTH." AND IT WAS SO.
GENESIS 1:11 ESV

As we grow up, every life experience, different challenges and seasons are the very seeds that are implanted in our hearts and minds, from which our character traits sprout and yield from. Everyone has good and bad seeds which makes us all diversely different and exquisitely unique. We do have our negative vines growing up in our hearts to deal with, from the hurt, injustice, ridicule and judgement we might have endured throughout our lifetime, letting bitterness settle in the deepest crevices of our being. If we leave it there, it will turn black, moldy and ugly and over time it will take root and be even more difficult to clean out. Forgiveness is like using the sharpest of spades along with a little salt! It gets down in the deepest, most inner parts, removing it all from the root. Forgiveness doesn't mean forgetting, but it does mean the beginning of letting go of the attached emotions to the offense and pushing on towards freedom from the weight of all that baggage we've been carrying around. I used to be so angry, I was happy on the outside to people I didn't know, but I could be so mean to my family that loved me. That anger was from years of unforgiveness and bitterness that stemmed from offense after offense I took all too personal. The abuse I endured had nothing to do with me and everything to do with them. We can keep ourselves from a lot of suffering if we could internalize three truths:

1. Hurting people hurt other people. It's not about you, it's about them and where they are in their journey. Don't take it personally, forgive, let it go and move on.
2. Where there is strife, there is someone's pride. The strongest isn't who wins the argument, the strongest is the first to concede and admit they are wrong and ask forgiveness.
3. Suffering is optional. If all else fails, speak to a pastor or trusted Christian mentor in your life. Read a book. The one that was life changing for me is "How to Stop the Pain" by Dr. James B. Richards.

We are all healing, just all at different stages of the process. The only normal people you know are the ones you don't know very well!

Wellness

Just ten minutes a day of exercise in physical motion can do incredible things, not only for your body but for your brain function as well! In just ten minutes, your muscles are signaling your brain you need more hormones to stir endurance, digestive enzyme production to burn more fuel and increased blood flow to move it all through your body to deliver what needs to be delivered. Ten Minutes doesn't require a trip to the gym or fancy workout clothes, just get moving and keep it going for ten minutes straight. My favorite is to turn on some really high energy music and just simply dance, sometimes holding five pound dumbbells in each hand. That little extra weight in your hands is doing wonders for your arm muscle tone as you wiggle your body and fling your arms to the music. Ten minutes a day, we are more likely to stick to it and do it every day. You are going to be shocked at the difference it will make!

Healthy

Essential oils are extracted from the concentrated properties of the healing components of plants, fruits and trees God has so plentifully given to us for all kinds of conditions. Oils for healing are mentioned in the Bible 188 times with the most famous being Frankincense and Myrrh the wise men brought as gifts for Jesus. I personally use Frankincense daily, not only in my skin care regimen but also Boswellia in supplement form. Do your research and select brands that offer 100 percent therapeutic grade oils and organic when available. Each oil has a specific purpose and can easily be incorporated in your daily routines.

Mirror Message of the Day

I am precious and honored in His sight and loved by my Father.
Isaiah 43:4

Notes

_____

_____

_____

_____

_____

_____

_____

_____

_____

_____

_____

_____

Day 12

"The Earth brought forth vegetation,
plants yielding seed according to their
own kinds, and trees bearing fruit in which
is their seed, each according to its own
kind. And God saw that it was good."
Genesis 1:12 ESV

Growing up left handed had its challenges but one thing is for sure, it provided for a wildly vivid imagination and definitely an artist's heart! In kindergarten I remember my teacher, Mrs. Bates telling my mom that my drawings were not normal, in a good way! I had drawn a horse and the detail of which I applied to my sketch apparently warranted attention, the wavy mane and flaring nostrils and so then it began. I continued in my art all through school, competing in local and national competitions and even attended an art camp in high school to nurture and develop my talent. Here's where I met Kara, she was a girl at my art camp from Baton Rouge, Louisiana and was all the things I ever dreamed I could be. She had the perfect teeny body, tanned skin, bluest eyes, southern drawl accent and the perfect wardrobe complete with the very most, coolest leather sandals I had ever seen! It was official, I wanted to be JUST LIKE HER! Once I was back home, I practiced styling my hair and makeup like her and adapted her style in my dress. I began pronouncing my words with her drawl and even found the exact same sandals! I burnt myself to a crisp that summer trying to achieve her tanned skin and ended up with a literal third degree burn on my chest from the sun. At the end of that eventful summer, I was still the same person, just pretending or putting on airs to be someone else, which proved not to work so well for me. God didn't design me to be Kara, He designed me to be me with all my flaws, quirky little idiosyncrasies and every mark of His beauty, reflecting in me. The Word says I am "fearfully and wonderfully made", unique and wonderful are His works! He has already planned each day, written in His book of life for me, hallelujah! Psalms 139:14 ESV How intricately magnificent are all His creations, from the tiniest seed to the most lavish of wonders, and each one of us are created in the same company and valued so far above all those things! Our beauty is within, and when we allow God to work His way in our life, we cannot help but find our outward shine.

Wellness

Stretching our muscles after exercise is such an essential and crucial way of increasing blood flow and increasing viability to those extreme digit parts that we tend to take for granted, our toes and fingers. Just think about all the ways fingers and toes are working during your workout, it is amazing! Static stretching, or maintaining a stretch longer than thirty seconds, is most effective as the longer you hold your stretch, the more increased flexibility you will have. You will find that maybe you cannot currently touch your toes, but consistently stretching will get you there in no time!

Healthy

Milk thistle. It is not just a weed growing in your yard, but a powerful medicinal that has been grown, harvested and used for its healing properties since the fourth century BC. It is available in several forms, powders, capsules and teas. It has been used for overall wellness, but its claim to fame is treating liver conditions. I began taking it when my gallbladder went south and still take it daily, because we all need a healthier liver so anything I can do to show it my love, I do. I use the powder form, 1/8 tsp combined with ½ tsp of Ceylon cinnamon added to my morning shake.

Mirror Message of the Day

I am filled with hope because my path has been established for a great future.
Jeremiah 29:11

Notes

Day 13

"And there was evening and there
was morning, the third day."
Genesis 1:13 ESV

The third day is critically significant for so many reasons. Day three is the day of resurrection, the day our Lord and Savior raised from the dead and fulfilled the promise of salvation for all of mankind that was, is and ever will be, hallelujah! The first person to see Jesus after the resurrection was Mary Magdalene, the woman Jesus healed from the bewitchment of sexual sin. She faithfully followed Jesus and the disciples as their caretaker. She was the first to see Him, because she was the first to show up.

In her obedience and faithfulness, she went to do the work, but when she arrived, the work was already done! God had already taken care of the work abundantly and beyond any expectation, leaving her only to bring glory to the highest name of Jesus. She resonated the miracle she had witnessed, proclaiming to the disciples the glorious wonder of promises fulfilled, to shout "look what God has done"! So often, if we will just be obedient to the promptings of the Holy Spirit and just show up to the place we need to be, we will find in God's faithfulness, the work is already complete. When God lays a certain person on your heart and you think, I really don't want to call, they will just complain and whine about how terrible everything is. Just do it, be the voice, be the friend that will just show up and be the shoulder to cry on. Let them know they are not alone in this journey. Show up and be the hands and feet of Jesus for them. You see lovelies, the work has already been done because He goes before us without fail and sets the stage. God is so faithful, let us be faithful and just show up.

Wellness

Gluteus Maximus, the name sounds intimidating, and along with its two counterparts, minimus and medius, they sound like this weekend's lineup on the WWF. They are actually our muscle trio that makes up our hind end, rear, buttocks, booty whatever you may call it, but it's actually the largest and heaviest muscle in the human body and supports our health in so many ways, and supports our ability to stand upright and left our legs to climb stairs. We know that large muscle groups help regulate metabolism so when we work out our gluteus muscles we are helping our body rev its engines and get going! A few easy ways to incorporate a quick and easy workout is to do back kicks as you brush your teeth, one minute for each leg. There are also great booty time workouts you can do in less than ten minutes a day you can find on social media or see my suggested work out in proceeding chapters.

Healthy

Cinnamon, it's delicious and the smell of it floods back childhood memories of cinnamon rolls our elementary school used to bake. Of course the Ceylon or true cinnamon I am talking about now is filled with a powerhouse of antioxidants your body will certainly thank you for. Just a quarter teaspoon a day, added to morning coffee or a shake can regulate blood sugar, reduce blood pressure, rev metabolism, reset insulin resistance, detox cells, and may prevent cancer growth. No wonder the Bible references its use in the company of the finest spices!

Mirror Message of the Day

I am far more precious than jewels.
Proverbs 31:10

_____

_____

_____

_____

_____

_____

_____

_____

_____

_____

_____

_____

Day 14

"And God said let there be lights in the
expanse of the heavens to separate the day
from the night. And let them be for signs
and for seasons, and for days and years,"
Genesis 1:14 ESV

There may be pain in the night, but joy comes in the morning. We go through seasons of growth, some rapid, some not so quick. I can remember waking up with pains in my legs, back and arms ... aches for no apparent reason, and my mom would always reassure me they are normal growing pains. You see, when we are in a fast growing period, it's uncomfortable and causes pain. It's how we respond to that pain that makes all the difference in the world. As I write this, I am in a season of growth and being stripped down. Through this, I tend to be moody, short tempered and not the most pleasant to be around. I know I must be careful and use caution with my words right now, remain calm and respond according to wisdom. I know that breakthrough is coming, I know God is doing a great work in me through all of this, so my prayer each morning has been, "Father God, please keep my hands from evil so that I may not do any harm." I take this from the prayer of Jabez found in I Chronicles 4:9-10. Jabez was a gimper for God, desiring to do more and more for Him. It's a powerful prayer I encourage everyone to pray daily. There is a book written by Dr. Bruce H Wilkinson called "The Prayer of Jabez ", that goes into great detail, describing how this simple little prayer completely changed and transformed his life and the life of so many over the course of thirty plus years of his ministry. I personally received this book as a gift for my fiftieth birthday, and began saying this prayer after completing it. Post it on your mirror that you will see it each morning as a reminder, set an alarm in your smartphone or make it part of your devotional time each day. I even suggest you re-read it again! Sometimes books influence us differently during chapters of our lives. We are rapidly growing, learning and walking an unknown path God is directing instead of going off all willy-nilly in our own direction. What an amazing journey if we will keep seeking the Father's plans, keep asking for the Holy Spirit's guidance, and keep confessing each victory comes from and passes through the Father's hands to you and me.

Wellness

Meditation on the Word of God opens new neural pathways in our minds, driving us towards joy, peace, tranquility and hope. In Psalms 119:148 ESV it says "My eyes are awake before the watches of the night, that I may meditate on your promise ..." We have all had those nights when we are wide awake and can't sleep because our brains will not stop replaying our day stories or we are thinking of the things we missed. I have often said that it is the Holy Spirit prompting us to pray, but after reading this scripture, we may be needing to meditate a new promise and write it deep in our innermost being. Write it deep in our hearts and meditate during those wakeful times. You just might be surprised by how quickly you will fall fast to sleep!

Healthy

Cilantro is not just for seasoning Mexican food, but has incredible healing properties that cleanse our bodies of the day to day garbage we pick up along the way. I call these types of foods magnets for they scavenge the body for heavy metals and will literally pull them out, releasing them through stool. It also protects our gut health with its powerful polyphenol concentration and antioxidants. It's antifungal, antibacterial and antiviral, helping to prevent food borne illnesses. This tiny little herb even has sedative properties that help reduce anxiety and improve sleep naturally. A great way I incorporate cilantro into my diet is by chopping the bundle up as soon as I get home from the grocery and store it in a freezer container. This preserves its freshness and makes it so convenient to throw on a salad or mix in with steamed veggies. If cooking with it, remember to add it last so all that good healing doesn't get cooked away!

Mirror Message of the Day

I am a prince/princess and heir to the throne of the one true King.
Psalms 45:13

Notes

Day 15

"AND LET THEM BE LIGHTS IN THE EXPANSE OF THE
HEAVENS TO GIVE LIGHT UPON THE EARTH", AND IT WAS SO.
GENESIS 1:15 ESV

Have you ever come home late and your home is pitch black inside? You grow a little anxious in finding the light switch and twink! Light floods into the room and all is right in the world again. There is such comfort found in light, in the warmth of it, where all things are exposed and seen as they are, fully illuminated. Numbers 6:25 ESV says "the LORD make his face shine on you and be gracious to you." Psalms 112:4 ESV says "Let Light shine out of the darkness" for the Godly. In Psalms 119:105 NKJV "Your Word is a lamp to my feet and a light to my path." Jesus Himself said "I am the light of the world." John 8:12 ESV It's been quite a few years since God showed me what it's like to walk in His light, and believe me, I spent a lot of years before that walking in the darkness of deception of culture. I used to think life was all about impressing this person or that person, not only with what I have but my knowledge and what social circles and company I keep. I thought my life purpose was to see how popular I could be and then social media was born. Oh wow, did that change things! Now I could measure how well liked I was by the number of "likes" I could get on a post. I would post something witty, or take a cute selfie and it was on. I would be checking to see how fast the tally went up. You see the most important growth and accomplishments in your life are the least recognized, the least praised, the least talked about and complimented. 1 Thessalonians 2:4 ESV says " ...we speak not to please man, but to please God who tests our hearts." The changes led by the Holy Spirit in compassion, giving, selflessness, humility and love are the everlasting imprints of our very being that transpose to not only beauty within, but radiates outward countenance in our very faces, causing our God lights to shine so bright. Others can't help but notice the change in us, asking us for our "secret sauce" and that's when your door is open to sharing all the goodness God has blessed you with and share your story. Not the social media kind, but the deep down, dirty, messy grime kind of reality of how God brought you to where you are. Joyce Meyer always says, "I may not be where I want to be, but I am sure not where I used to be." Keep moving forward beautiful, keep growing, keep letting God shine that ever glowing, brilliant light through you!

Wellness

Strength training, through lifting even minimal weights, is beneficial in so many different ways. Our skeletal-muscle system begins to shrink and decline as we age, so working out muscle groups and increasing strength is critical to metabolism as it revs your resting metabolic rate. So even when you are stationary, you are still burning fat and calories providing your body with the increased absorption of all of those great nutrients you have been feeding it, in turn having more energy and positive moods. Also, you are increasing protection of your bones which keeps us more viable as we age, preventing injuries to joints. I recommend starting out by adding five pound weights to your current work out and work your way up as the added weight becomes easier during your exercise. If you find that holding weights in your hands is an awkward addition, they make strap on weights for your wrists and ankles that may be more comfortable.

Healthy

Coconut Oil has become a staple in our home and stands in light company of other oils in our pantry. I cook everything in it, I even use it for butter on my sprouted toasted muffins, yum! I cannot begin to describe countless improvements to my family's health since making this switch. Coconut Oil helps regulate blood sugar, improve mental alertness, lower bad cholesterol, boost heart health and so much more! I urge you to throw out and be done with that shortening, canola oil, vegetable oil, corn oil, sunflower oil, safflower oil and stick to the cold pressed, unrefined, organic delicious goodness of coconut oil!

Mirror Message of the Day

I am a new creation in Christ, all of my old ways are passed away.
II Corinthians 5:17

Notes

_____

_____

_____

_____

_____

_____

_____

_____

_____

_____

_____

Day 16

"THEN GOD MADE TWO GREAT LIGHTS; THE
GREATER LIGHT TO RULE THE DAY, AND THE
LESSER LIGHT TO RULE THE NIGHT."
GENESIS 1:16 NKJV

Today, time springs forward and all are buzzing about whether we should do away with daylight savings time. Here in the US there are several states that do not recognize the time changes anymore. What it comes down to is one simple fact, we do not like change. I'm personally a creature of habit and get stuck in patterns of repeat, for instance when we go out to dinner, I order the same thing, every time, all the time. When I get ready for work in the morning, I do things in a set sequence of events, because I reason in my mind I have timed each task and if I vary, I risk running late. Change is incredibly difficult, as our brains literally form pathways of repetition from our habits created over the years called Neural Pathways. Those Neural Pathways have to be completely re-wired and re-written in order for new habits to form. To break free from the societal influences and pressures to be like everyone else, let us focus on what God has called us to do and that's not be transformed to this world. In Romans 12:2 ESV it says for us to "be transformed by the RENEWAL of your mind, that by testing you may discern what is the will of God, what is good and acceptable and perfect". So how do we do this? Let's say every time I am in traffic I become frustrated with the drivers around me and before long, I am honking, breaking heavy and yelling that I can't stand people! I am thinking God is not pleased with this series of events and the hateful yuck that just came out of my mouth! I cannot change the way other drivers drive, so the only way to see a change is to change me, re-write my response, re-calculate my reaction, shift my paradigm. Let's examine and find the root cause, which in this case is fear. Fear led to the anxiousness in driving, my mind perceiving danger in the way others were driving around me. To overcome fear, my favorite truth scripture is II Timothy 1:7 NKJV "For God has not given us a spirit of fear, but of power, and of love and of a sound mind." I will speak it out loud, listen to praise and worship, listen to my favorite pastor's messages and begin to rewrite that response! I will, only through the power of Jesus, change me. It's not easy to change our set ways of response and thinking, but if we press forward with God, all things are possible! If you consistently correct your thoughts with His promises, it will not be long until one day you are driving along and someone pulls in front of you and instead of getting upset, you are actually thankful they didn't hit you and amazed at your calm. That's the power of God working in you!

Wellness

Smart watches and fitness trackers are all the rave right now. I have to admit, having owned and used them daily for the last four years is a game changer for my physical activity. The idea is to accomplish ten thousand steps by the end of the day, and I was shocked at how easily attainable that goal is! Those ten thousand steps burn five hundred calories and reinforce the great metabolic change in our bodies that only comes from consistent, daily activity. You will begin to experience increased energy, improved digestion, cardiac health, blood pressure and A1C levels will begin to drop. At your next yearly physical your doctor will be asking you for health advice because of all this work you are doing to optimize your health and the great awakening and transformation in you!

Healthy

I am not a huge fan of supplements in pill or capsule form, but there are a few that are incredibly important for our bodies to have in abundance, daily. Among the top of the essential list is a good B complex. The series of

B vitamins are responsible for such a plethora of functions from digestion to brain health, to muscle strength and metabolism. Each morning I take a good, clean organic B complex that is derived from food sources and doesn't contain the added icks that come along with most supplements on the market. Be careful to read your labels and steer clear of those dirty dozen additives we talked about in previous chapters. It's amazing the clarity you will begin to feel in just a few, short days after.

Mirror Message of the Day

I am provided all my needs, eat, drink and clothing from my Father in Heaven. Matthew 6:31-33

Notes

Day 17

"God set them in the firmament of the
heavens to give light on the earth,"
Genesis 1:17 NKJV

We are called to be a walking, living, breathing testimony of God's power and love. Each one of us strategically placed where we are today for His purposes, just as He appointed each star in the heavens where it is. What better way to witness to someone in the power of God, but to show His power in our choices and how we respond to life circumstances.

If we try hard enough, everything we do can be justified to an extent to help make it acceptable in our minds, doesn't mean it's right, just justified in our own thoughts. That's exactly how the enemy works to blind us to sin, so if we are not careful, we can run ourselves right into a rut and keep cutting that groove deeper and deeper until the only way to get out is for God Himself to pick us up and out of it. That rut isn't formed overnight, it's something we don't even realize is happening until the rut is already forming, like a dog running a fence line. It's the day in, day out small compromises we accept and that slow fade into allowing emotionally led tidbits of desire, jealousy, resentment, selfishness, unforgiveness to move into our hearts and minds. That's why it is so important to pray and hear the word daily, read the word daily, speak the word daily because it is the Word that draws us out of that rut, and sets us on the solid ground of truth. In Proverbs 3:6 NLT the Word says "Seek His will in all you do, and He will show you which path to take." The more connected to God we become the louder we hear His still small voice and the more we heed and surrender to His direction, the more we will prosper in our relationship with God and He can take us so much farther and beyond anything we could imagine. Ephesians 3:20 NKJV says He will do "exceedingly abundantly" above all we ask or think, so that definitely excites me for what is to come.

Wellness

I have worn makeup for the last thirty-eight years, but did not start washing my face before bed in a regular nighttime regimen, until I was thirty-five years old. Had I known in my teens what I know today about skincare, I would have started much earlier in life! The revelation came when examining my face closely in a magnifying mirror of a hotel we stayed in on a family vacation that year. To my surprise, I found small little ruts, lines and crevices forming around my eyes, mouth and between my eyes. My disciplined nighttime, skin pampering began that very evening, and continues to this very day. I wash my face with baby wash and moisturize with jojoba, rose and frankincense essential oils, that's it! Jojoba is the closest, natural oil that matches the oils our skin produces, rose and frankincense have healing properties to nourish my skin from the outside in. They sell a cold pressed, organic jojoba in a six ounce bottle that typically lasts me six months or more, super inexpensive. Rose and Frankincense are a little costly, but last about six months as well, and still way less expensive than most fancy facial skin care products, plus all natural and organic.

Healthy

Super green powders are a staple in my diet and so easy to add to my morning shake. It is an acquired taste, but with the amount of fruit and added goodies my shakes contain, it's actually hard to distinguish the taste of them. The benefit of adding a greens powder is that right in that teaspoon serving are four to five servings of powerhouse green micronutrients your body will thank you for. The one I currently use is certified organic and has a blend of wheatgrass, barley grass, baobab, moringa, spirulina and chlorella, so good! All of these glorious components work inside your body to reduce inflammation, super boost immunity, cleanse and detoxify by working both as a warrior food and magnet food. It will not take long to feel the benefits!

Mirror Message of the Day

I am given a straight path to walk my future in Christ Jesus.
Proverbs 3:5-6

Notes

_____

_____

_____

_____

_____

_____

_____

_____

_____

_____

_____

Day 18

"AND TO RULE OVER THE DAY AND OVER THE
NIGHT, AND TO DIVIDE THE LIGHT FROM THE
DARKNESS. AND GOD SAW THAT IT WAS GOOD."
GENESIS 1:18 NKJV

Sometimes, I can be so exhausted from the day, my body just screams to
get deep transcending sleep, so I strategically plan the rude awakening of
my alarm for a minimum sleep of seven hours, my optimum sleep cycle …
Slipping into my well-made bed, I snuggle down and settle in and BAM!
EYES WIDE OPEN! Suddenly my brain is bursting with thoughts of
everything I didn't do that needed done and every response played out
differently in my brain, out of all times, why now? The what if I would
have, or I should have said, and did I smile or was I rude? Bah!! Clearly,
it's dark outside, clearly my mind should know what my body has been
telling me for hours, its sleep time instead of replaying scenarios in my
head. This is when I pray … there must be some reason, something I
missed or someone God is laying on my heart to pray for. Two minutes
later and a simple prayer; "Father God, search my heart … please reveal
to me anything I may be holding in my heart, I need to lay down at your
feet, reveal to me anyone that needs specific prayer or has needs. In Jesus'
name, amen." Just like that, God will faithfully bring to my mind the most
random people or a situation where I was less than gracious in my words
or actions and need to ask forgiveness. It seems almost instantly once the
words or thoughts leave me, I am out, sound asleep. Having a little talk
with Jesus is the most effective sleep aid ever! When I was little, I would
sing "Jesus Loves Me" and this is something I passed on to all three of my
children. I assure you, the last thing the enemy wants to hear is you singing

that classic profession of Jesus' love for you because the Bible tells us so. You will conk out, lickety split! When God tells us in His Word to pray about everything, He means everything, even the small stuff.

Wellness

Bedtime yoga is a great way to relax your mind and body in preparation of a restful night's sleep. YouTube is full of instruction videos you can use until you develop your own personal routine. Time ranges from fifteen minutes to as little as five minutes to reap the benefits associated with the practice of yoga. When performing a few simple yoga exercises in the comfort of your bed, you are increasing blood flow, reducing anxiety, boosting hormone production and so much more! Those few minutes you spend each night will yield hours of peace filled restful sleep.

Healthy

When I first was diagnosed with Hashimoto's I began researching all of the natural supplements that would increase my thyroid hormone production and at the top of every list I found was Ashwagandha. It's such a funny little word for such a powerful force. It is clinically proven to lower cortisol levels, making it a great stress buster and sleep promoter. Ashwagandha has been used for centuries in Ayurvedic medicine to lower blood pressure, reduce inflammation, defend against cancer, regulate blood sugar and has even been used as an antidepressant. This ground root, often called Indian Ginseng is available in powder form or capsulized in a gelatin capsule. I choose the capsules because the powder has such a strong putrid taste, it could alter the taste of my shakes. Of course, as always, talk to your physician before beginning any supplements.

Mirror Message of the Day

I am equipped with the light of life in Christ Jesus and will never walk in darkness.
John 8:12

Notes

_____

_____

_____

_____

_____

_____

_____

_____

_____

_____

_____

_____

Day 19

"AND THERE WAS EVENING AND THERE
WAS MORNING, THE FOURTH DAY."
GENESIS 1:19 ESV

Lazarus was Mary and Martha's brother we read about in John 11. This scripture talks about how he grew ill while Jesus was away from Bethany, where they resided and could not make the journey in time before he passed. As Jesus neared the city, Lazarus had been in the tomb for four days already, but told Martha that her brother would rise again. Martha ran to tell Mary and when she heard the news, ran to Jesus and led him to Lazarus' tomb. Jesus spoke to Lazarus, calling him by name and said "Lazarus, come forth". John 11:43 NKJV On that fourth day, the Bible says that Jews believed Jesus was who He said He was. Lives were changed and chains of bondage of disbelief were broken on that day. In Hebrew the number four means "appointed time" and I believe that God's timing is always spot on. Day four of Lazarus being in the grave was significant to the Jews in being present, standing with Mary in witness of the wondrous miracle of Lazarus' resurrection from the tomb.

Our lives today are filled with divine appointments in our daily run-abouts, errands and even our professional life. I meet with people daily with a plethora of personalities, economical background and ethnicity. My desire each day is to represent Jesus well in my words, actions and mannerisms, allowing Him to shine through me because I never know when any given meeting just might be an appointed time orchestrated by the Father of Lights. An opportunity for me to share a little glimpse of my heart and love of the Father. In Hebrews 13:2 ESV it says; "Do not neglect to show hospitality to strangers, for thereby some have entertained angels unawares." We never know how those simple little acts of kindness could impact someone so it's important to always be kind and do good.

Wellness

"Brusha, brusha, brusha …" Growing up, this little song was my cue to brush my teeth and I have passed that little ditty along to my children and to their children. Dental hygiene is among the most important to maintain overall wellness. It is quite literally the front door to your entire body. It is extremely important to brush at least twice a day and floss before bed to ensure your mouth is free from food and bacteria that cause decay as you sleep. In addition, visit a fluoride free, homeopathic dentist twice a year for those cleanings and gum health checks. Fluoride is an outdated application in dental care that wrecks more havoc in the body than it could ever help, so my suggestion is always fluoride free everything. Opt for toothpaste with a charcoal base for super whitening and detox twice a week.

Healthy

Unless your daily diet is extremely balanced with plenty of animal protein and leafy green veggies, you are most likely missing out on some essential B vitamins for so many processes throughout your body. All of the B vitamins are water soluble so what you don't need, your body expels through waste, so taking a B complex supplement is highly recommended. Most importantly, B's are essential in converting the food you eat into energy throughout the day to keep you moving. It is also critical in the production of hormones to keep those moody blues at bay, especially premenstrual syndrome. When taking B complex, you are supporting your overall health, including brain function and cell regeneration. Always check your supplements for the dirty dozen and make sure your brand is third party tested and certified free of all the junk you don't want or need, ever.

Mirror Message of the Day

I am filled with peace, I will not be afraid or let my heart be troubled. John 14:27

Notes

_____

_____

_____

_____

_____

_____

_____

_____

_____

_____

_____

_____

_____

Day 20

"AND GOD SAID, "LET THE WATERS SWARM WITH SWARMS
OF LIVING CREATURES, AND LET BIRDS FLY ABOVE THE
EARTH ACROSS THE EXPANSE OF THE HEAVENS."
GENESIS 1:20 ESV

Swarm with swarms ... this paints a picture in my mind of the oceans being so filled with ocean life, there would hardly be room to swim, bountiful sea creatures of every kind pushing and jumping up, in and out of the water. What a miraculous wonder to have witnessed the creation of living, breathing creatures populating the world's oceans and skies for the first time! I fully expect once I'm in heaven, to be able to view rewinds and replay of the whole thing. He does everything exceedingly and abundantly above and beyond what we could imagine and that's what I see here, Father God creating in abundance overflowing and pouring out of the banks. Jesus filled John and Simon Peter's nets so full, they couldn't lift them, the five loaves and two fishes feeding 5,000 with twelve bushels filled and overflowing left over, Water turned to wine at a wedding Jesus attended with cups and vessels pouring over. These are all perfect examples of the loving generosity of our Father God, and the overwhelming goodness He desires to bless each one of His beloved children with. Sweethearts, we worship that same God today who powered the miracles we see here, along with so many countless others and He never stops being that same God, that same Abba Father. James 1:17 NIV says "Every good and perfect gift is from above, coming down from the Father of the heavenly lights, who does NOT change like shifting shadows." He is constant, steady, stable, unmoving and never failing. That same abundance He gave on the fifth day of creation in filling the waters and skies, is the same abundance of grace, mercy, lovingkindness, provision, protection and wisdom He will give us when we call on His name.

Wellness

One of my favorite things to do is gather my family of adult children together with their children for dinner just so we can all spend some quality time. This communion and camaraderie is quite literally food for this momma's soul, it lifts up my joy to see all my children laughing together, sharing stories, reminiscing and telling what's going on in their lives right now. Our minds, bodies and heart need that connection to feel united, interwoven in love and know we always have a safe place to go called home. Just a few of the top physical benefits are improved mental health, stress reduction, boost to our self-confidence and increased life expectancy. If you live somewhere distant and don't have family close, gather your friends in the same manner. Go ahead, be the catalyst to your next gathering, set those new traditions and start strengthening those bonds of love.

Healthy

Iodine is crucial in the healthy function of the thyroid gland and production of hormones vital for proper organ support. I choose to supplement to ensure I get my daily dose because I do not eat enough iodine rich foods in my diet. I take Sea Kelp because it's a naturally derived rich source of iodine and because it's "food" it is much more bioavailable for my body. Be sure to speak to your doctor before supplementing and do not exceed 150 mcg daily to avoid overload and storing excessive amounts. If you are getting your daily amount in your diet, then supplementing may not be necessary for you. Benefits include, healthy thyroid function, improved cognitive health and energy.

Mirror Message of the Day

I am favored by Father God and have good success because I have written
His love and faithfulness on the table of my heart.
Proverbs 3:7-8

Notes

Day 21

"So God created the great sea creatures
and every living creature that moves, with
which the waters swarm, according to their
kinds, and every winged bird according to
its kind. And God saw that it was good."
Genesis 1:21 ESV

One of my favorite places to go is the zoo and has been since I was little. I adore animals, all kinds of animals and actually went to college to become a zoologist. I was even offered a position as curator of Reptilia at our city zoo, but then he told me the salary and yeah, that was not going to come close to paying the bills for myself and my three children, so I declined. Each year as the kids grew up, we would renew our zoo friend membership, a one year open pass to go any time we wanted. All three of my adult children now love the zoo just as much as I do and we enjoy our zoo time with the grands. This is my way of imparting my passion for these glorious creatures on to our next generation! Legacy living in the making is a beautiful thing and the zoo is just a tiny snippet of all the wondrous wonders in store for them as they grow. I am confident their Papa and I will get to impart to each of them all the things life robs us from teaching our own children until we've circled around a couple of mountains and walked a few low valleys with Jesus by our side. Psalms 91:16 ESV says "With long life I will satisfy him and show him my salvation". You see, every encounter, adventure, and appointment makes up the composition of your life experience and your reaction and how you choose to respond. Every minute, every hour of every day is the secret sauce to who you are. Our life story is filled with choices and lessons from them, but we learn best listening to wisdom gained from others in positions of influence like parents, grandparents, church mentors because chances are, they have walked out the same stuff at one time or another and have the best advice. Proverbs 8:11 ESV says "wisdom is better than jewels, and all that you may desire cannot compare with her." Wisdom is the true gift of legacy, the most abundant and valuable inheritance you could ever obtain, and Father God gives it freely beyond measure just for asking.

Wellness

We have all heard the saying "Laughter is the best medicine". Well now there is science to back up that claim and most importantly, the Word declares that very same; "Then our mouth was filled with laughter, and our tongue with shouts of joy; then they said among the nations, "The Lord has done great things for them." Psalm 126:2 ESV When we laugh, our brain releases endorphins that not only boost our mood but act as a pain reliever, lower stress responses and can even work as an anti -inflammatory. Laughing between friends and family creates bonds of kinship relationally. I've even shared laughs with a complete stranger before and immediately feel that same human connection that only comes out from the depths of our hearts. Laughter lets us know we are still able to have hope, we are still able to experience joy in the midst of array circumstances. With all of these incredible benefits, let's do our best to keep each other laughing.

Healthy

On a smoldering hot summer day, there is nothing quite as refreshing as a tall glass of cool water. Growing up, we would all gather around to get our turn sipping up the water out of the garden hose like it was liquid gold! We all need water in generous amounts every day, from the time we wake up to the time we go to bed, I get it, it's hard to remember to drink all that water throughout the day, but dehydration slows your metabolism and interferes with our cellular functions that are critical to our health, so this is best avoided. Always have clean filtered water or a good quality spring water at your disposal throughout the day. Try setting reminders on your phone or using a water drinking app that prompts you to drink water consistent all day.

Mirror Message of the Day

I am refreshed and healed in my bones because I worship the Lord God and trust in His wisdom.
Proverbs 3:7-8

Notes

_____

_____

_____

_____

_____

_____

_____

_____

_____

_____

_____

Day 22

AND GOD BLESSED THEM, SAYING, "BE FRUITFUL
AND MULTIPLY, AND FILL THE WATERS IN THE SEAS,
AND LET BIRDS MULTIPLY ON THE EARTH."
GENESIS 1:22 NKJV

Adults ask kids all the time what they want to be when they grow up and even children of very early ages already have a pretty good idea! I can remember wanting to be an astronaut, then a scientist, a horse trainer, a karate instructor and the list goes on and on. With each passing fancy I would have, my mom and dad would make sure I had plenty of books to read up on each one and wholeheartedly encouraged my passions. I look back at those times and realize they were creating legacy, they were building and shaping my future in ways their parents didn't or were not able to. I see now this was their increase, their fruit, their way of adding more to the melting pot of humans in this world in making me more confident, loved and focused than either one received from their parents, and my grandparents increased in their rearing of my parents, looking back in reverse. Raising and taking care of a child is one of the most incredibly joyous and jubilant experiences while all together terrifying and painful. Without God's strength, grace and daily doses of mercy, I'm not sure how any parent survives! There are so many moments while raising my three littles, I look back and can clearly see the hand of God guiding, directing and working each circumstance together for benefit to enrich our lives, even though at the time we felt like it would be the end of us. In writing this, I called my mom just to tell her how much I appreciate all my dad and her did for me and her response was "Oh darlin', it was all God's doing! I give Him all the credit!" Her words massaged my heart and penetrated deep within me. This is legacy, this is humility in knowing God's goodness and strength at work through each one of us to do all we are called to be; all we are called to do. There will always be times we will think it's the end, just know we may not see or feel the presence of Jesus with us, but He's there, holding our right hand as we keep moving forward.

Wellness

I have the distinct privilege of caring for my granddaughter every other Wednesday while my daughter works. This day has been deemed "Mimi Day" and we have the best adventures! We frequent the zoo or go to parks, the aquarium and sometimes just hang around the house, but always on the move, up and down off the floor, running, jumping and playing! The next day I feel like I just spent the day at the gym, as every muscle in my body, some I didn't know existed, hurt. Not only does this time benefit me physically, the mental rewards for this time spent results in precious memories that will be carried and cherished for the rest of days. If you do not have children or grands, you could always volunteer at your church nursery or local YMCA. A very wise influence in my life told me to always smile at a child, because that simple act of kindness provides hope of love for their future.

Healthy

Turmeric, a beautifully hued, rich spice with the warmest taste has been tops in the health headlines for the last few years. It is commonly used in Ayurvedic medicine for centuries with the health benefits being so incredibly vast for the human body. I truly believe Turmeric is a God given cure for so many ailments, containing Curcumin with its powerful anti-inflammatory properties, it can be used daily in fighting cancer, SIBO, diabetes, Alzheimer's, Parkinson's, arthritis. Turmeric can even be used to whiten teeth! Each morning I take a gelatin capsule supplement with turmeric and use a quarter to half a teaspoon in my veggie sauté' several times a week. When cooking with Turmeric, it is important to combine with cayenne or black pepper to increase its bioavailability along with coconut oil to serve as a carrier to push all the goodness throughout your system.

Mirror Message of the Day

I am forgiven and my wrongdoings and sin are never remembered again by my Father in Heaven.
Hebrews 8:12

Notes

_____

_____

_____

_____

_____

_____

_____

_____

_____

_____

_____

_____

_____

Day 23

"AND THERE WAS EVENING AND THERE
WAS MORNING, THE FIFTH DAY."
GENESIS 1:23 ESV

Every morning, I wake up earlier than I need to so I have this time to devote to God, prayer, the word and writing. I am such the creature of habit, almost to a fault because when my time is interrupted, it is very upsetting to me and I have a tendency to not be very nice about it. Right now, during the pandemic, my husband is working from home and let's just say we have been spending a lot of time together in the morning, early, every day. I'm doing my best to adapt to the current circumstance, making light of him being in my space. It hasn't really not bothered me, until he decided the dogs should also be up with us that early in the morning. That was it, this was the straw! You see, the fifth day is the day of grace and it's time to grow mine. John 1:16 NIV says "Out of His fullness we have all received grace in place of grace already given."

I cried out to God; "I want normal back" and in that still small voice, He answered, "Really? What is normal to you?" After some time and meditation in the Word, this was my reply;

"*Normal* does not belong to me. I gave my life to you Father, committed my steps to your purpose, opened my heart to Your Word, this life is not mine but Yours. Thank you for reminding me today my strength, wisdom, power, grace, mercy and love is from You alone and without You, I can do NOTHING, I am NOTHING, but with YOU, I am EVERYTHING You designed me to be and it's so much more exceedingly and abundantly more than I could have ever imagined!" Ephesians 3:20 NKJV tells us, confirms for us this; "Now to Him who is able to do exceedingly abundantly above all that we ask or think, according to the power that works in us." Let it be, Father. Let it be.

Wellness

Our days are filled with opportunities to increase our physical activity as we do our day in, day out regular stuff. When we wake in the morning, start with deep breaths followed by stretching to help jumpstart circulation. When parking your car for shopping or to go to a place of business, don't choose princess parking, but park further out to increase your steps for the day. If you have a choice at work or elsewhere you frequent, take the stairs instead of the elevator. Carry your own groceries to your car and into your home. Take a few five minute breaks during the day to stand up and do twenty jumping jacks, or toe touches. These are simple little things you can do and can have such an impact on your overall wellness.

Healthy

In my world, food is medicine and as you know by now I like to naturally obtain the majority of my supplements through herbs, nuts, grains, fruit, and veggies. One nutrient critical in the healing and maintenance of Hashimotos or any disorder of the thyroid is Selenium. If you are taking a multivitamin, you are more than likely consuming plenty, but if you are limiting your intake of manufactured supplements, Brazil Nuts are the quickest and easiest way to get your daily requirement. I eat one a day, providing me with up to ninety-one mcg of selenium, where the recommended daily allowance is sixty mcg. Selenium is critical in regulating your hormone production, and your body's natural production of glutathione, our immune system's super hero. I use Terrasoul Superfoods organic raw brazil nuts and keep them in the refrigerator after opening. Do not exceed one or two nuts a day, as always, too much of a good thing can be counterproductive, even detrimental to your health.

Mirror Message of the Day

I am satisfied and replenished when my soul grows weary, through my Father God.
Jeremiah 31:25

Notes

_____

_____

_____

_____

_____

_____

_____

_____

_____

_____

_____

_____

Day 24

"THEN GOD SAID, "LET THE EARTH BRING FORTH THE
LIVING CREATURE ACCORDING TO ITS KIND; CATTLE
AND CREEPING THING AND THE BEAST OF THE EARTH,
EACH ACCORDING TO ITS KIND"; AND IT WAS SO.
GENESIS 1:24 NKJV

Growing up, one of my children's favorite books was "A Million Chameleons" by James Young. It's a whimsical book filled with adventures for these colorful little chameleons as they dance, rhyme, play and change their colors on each page. The last two pages illustrate all of the chameleons in multiple shades of every hue imaginable! This book was definitely one of the most requested at story time and still brings smiles to my heart. I've known a few people in my time that have what I call Chameleon personalities, remodeling from one color to being a chameleon of another color, depending on whom they are with. Suddenly, their likes, interests, beliefs and ideas change as a way of impressing or pleasing others and contorting who they are to be more compatible. God made each one of us to be as unique as each intricate snowflake formed in the snowy winter sky, no two are ever alike. Consider our fingerprints, our DNA is never identical to another human, not even between identical twins, that's how uniquely created we are. In Matthew 10:30 NIV the Word says each hair on our heads is numbered. WOW! Can you imagine? That's how much the Father cares for you. This is the great extent of how precious you are to Him, set apart as His treasured masterpiece, His child created for such a spectacular plan He has written just for you. This world deserves to meet the real you because your purpose and the plan God has for you requires it, not the masks of insecurity, fear, shame and doubt that you wear. It's time to clean out the closet of all the colored masks you've collected over the years, throw them out and burn them, because you don't need them anymore. God's about to show you just who you really are as soon you just ask in the name of Jesus, let it be so. Darling, you are fearfully and wonderfully made, from before the time you were formed in your mother's womb, and your story is already written. (Psalms 139:14) Just like that, your heart and mind will begin to be saturated with your true colors, bursting out like a rainbow shining through for all to see!

Wellness

I read a quote the other day and it said "There are two types of tired; one that requires rest and one that requires peace." This little statement rang so loud and true to my heart because we all get tired. Even Jesus grew tired. John 4:6 NIV. Whether that tiredness is physical or mental, we need to listen to our bodies and succumb to which enlivening we need. It's amazing what a fifteen minute "pause" will do, even five minutes to look up and say, "Father, I surrender it all to you, my life, relationships, thoughts, and words, all of it. Jesus, thank you for giving me this gift and making it possible to be still and rest in Your name … Jesus." Then drink it all in, drink in that living water that can only come from the well of life, that one source that never fails, the name of Jesus. Pause, and find your calm.

Healthy

Another star ingredient in my morning shakes is finely ground flax seed. The health benefits resulting from a tablespoon a day is astounding, but the three top are its omega 3, lignins and fiber content. Just this one little serving a day is helping my body prevent cancer, regulate hormone production and receptors and keeping my gut healthy and happy, moving everything along nice and regular. Flax seed can also regulate sugar, and reduce high blood pressure. Flax seeds can be purchased whole, but our digestive systems have a really difficult time breaking them down to reap all the goodness that we could if it is finely ground.

Mirror Message of the Day

I have eternal life, I dwell in the hand of my Father in Heaven and no one can remove me.
John 10:28

Notes

_____

_____

_____

_____

_____

_____

_____

_____

_____

_____

_____

_____

Day 25

"AND GOD MADE THE BEASTS OF THE EARTH
ACCORDING TO THEIR KINDS, AND EVERYTHING
THAT CREEPS ON THE EARTH ACCORDING TO ITS
KIND. AND GOD SAW THAT IT WAS GOOD."
GENESIS 1:25 NKJV

When my oldest son was little, he grew fascinated with dinosaurs so I bought for him a book, a huge encyclopedia edition that was filled with these brilliantly colored creatures illustrating each kind and labeled with detailed descriptions. He determined to learn the facts listed for each one, what they ate, where they lived and how they inhibited, creeped and roamed this earth. That book was almost bigger than him and we would read it together every day, one dinosaur at a time. Exploring each kind, it was obvious the care our Father took in creating them so unique and intricately detailed. I truly believe there were dinosaurs on Noah's Ark (Genesis 8:19), and why they did not survive will be a question reserved for God, added to the list of "why" questions stockpiled in my mental filing cabinet, to personally address when my time Earth side is complete. The Word says there is a season, and a time for every matter under heaven (Ecclesiastes 3:1 ESV), and I believe God has His reasons for dinosaurs becoming extinct. Wouldn't it be cool if He said, they lived because I wanted my children to enjoy their fantastical splendor, just for pure joy. King Solomon wrote a little further along that "He (God) has made everything beautiful in its time. Also, He has put eternity into a man's heart, yet so that he cannot find out what God has done from the beginning to the end." Ecclesiastes 3:11 ESV There is nothing better for us to do than to be joyful and do good, because all of this is our gift from God. Each day, each experience, each breath are all a gift from God for our delight and our pleasure. Let's be mindful of the little God winks along our path today, a beautiful sunrise, a little flower growing in the most unexpected place or that random act of kindness from a complete stranger. These are all things that bring us such joy and all these things are an absolute gift from God. Just remember, you will always find what your heart seeks.

Wellness

I am a firm believer that our human mind needs a break every once and awhile from reality and just engage in something that stimulates our thought processes. Some use crossword puzzles or find a word, but then smartphones were born and everyone started playing solitaire, remember that? Now, I play Candy Crush and currently on level 3025. Its colorful funny pieces, problem solving puzzles and obstacles entertain a good fifteen minutes at a time, methodically clearing the boards of jellies and bombs. I have noticed that jigsaw puzzles are trending right now, with their beautiful graphics and photography as a reward at the end, plugging that last piece of puzzle in. Exercising our brains is just as important in keeping healthy as exercising our bodies.

Healthy

"Bu-nanas!" Bananas have always been a staple in our family, God's perfect little on the go snack is small, compact, delicious and complete in its own packaging and has a built in handle to keep little hands clean. Considered a superfood, it is rich with vitamin C, B6, Potassium, bromelain, manganese, magnesium, fiber and tryptophan for that feel good and restful sleep. At different levels of ripening of a banana, the sugars and fiber change, and can be healing for certain ailments like digestion and even cancer. The less ripe, or more green a banana can aid in digestion, and the more ripe, or more bright yellow and forming a few brown spots on the skin indicates when it is great to restore glycogen and electrolytes. Bananas can be frozen to lock them at certain stages to be used in smoothies or shakes.

You can even make super rich and healthy ice cream treats from frozen bananas. Yum!!

Mirror Message of the Day

I am loved by God before the creation of the world, He blessed me and prepared for me my place.
Matthew 25:34

Notes

Day 26

"Then God said, "Let us make man in our image, after our likeness. And let them have dominion over the fish of the sea and over the birds of the heavens and over the livestock and over all the earth and over every creeping thing that creeps on the earth."
Genesis 1:26 ESV

When I consider the image of God, I see Him as the most pure form of love we can fathom, love so divine, love so beyond perfect. And just like that, man was made in the image of God, and God gave everything He just spoke into creation over to his stewardship, his care and his protection. It completely shook my entire core when I had the revelation of the first gesture of love He gave to man, the first gift was relinquishing all the majestic wonders of this Earth He had literally just created, pure and undefiled. Is it even possible for me to articulate the magnitude and vastness of the Father's love for us? The apostle John must have had this same revelation because in his gospel, he mentions the word love fifty-seven times and another forty-six times in the first epistle of John! Let's not forget that he always referred to himself as the disciple Jesus loved. This isn't John being arrogant or presumptuous, but a man who was confident and filled with the faith in KNOWING who he was in Christ Jesus, knowing his worth as a child of God. He got it, he completely understood his purpose in creation. Among my favorite verses is 1 John 4:19 NIV "We love because He first loved us." Scholars for years have pondered what set John apart with Jesus, why did Jesus favor John so much, but here's the key; in Acts 10:34 KJV the Word says God is not a respecter of persons; He does not show favoritism from one to another. So why is John called the disciple

Jesus loved six times in the book of John? John wrote the book of John! John is calling himself the "disciple Jesus loved". You see beautiful, God loves you the same amount today, as yesterday and will love you tomorrow as much as He does today. His love is a steadfast love and we are all just as special, just as loved, just as precious to our Father as the best Christian you know. Once you are able to grasp the full completeness of Father God's love for you, then you are set free to love yourself. He loves you so much that He sent His only begotten Son, that whosoever believeth on Him should not perish, but have everlasting life. John 3:16 KJV

Wellness

Proper posture is a lost art that I haven't seen taught since I was a child, however is incredibly important to our everyday and future health. The benefits of maintaining proper posture while sitting, standing and walking can make all the difference in preserving our joint health, reduce headaches, increase lung capacity, improve circulation and aid in digestion. With proper posture contributing so many positives to our well-being, let's be mindful of how we hold our bodies and not slump through the day, rise up straight to take in all the beauty we see when we look up and take notice, so one day the view our of shoes isn't the only thing in our line of vision.

Healthy

When I was growing up in the seventy's, grapefruit diets were all the rave and my mom made sure I had my half of a grapefruit before every meal. It was theorized that grapefruit could speed your metabolism, increasing weight loss. Grapefruit is amazingly good for you, but eating one and a half a day is a little over the top. I use grapefruit in my fruit diet rotation about once or twice a week to benefit from the digestive enzymes present. The antioxidants found in grapefruit are perfect for giving your immune system a super boost along with the high levels of vitamin C. Caution must be taken with taking prescription medications known to have adverse interactions with grapefruit. Check with your doctor before incorporating it in your diet.

Mirror Message of the Day

I am strong in the Lord and His great power.
Ephesians 6:10

Notes

Day 27

"So God created man in his own image,
in the image of God he created him;
male and female he created them."
Genesis 1:27 ESV

I've often said Adam and Eve had it so easy, God took Adam and said BAM! Here you go! This is your significant other, with no leftover baggage from broken relationships, no wounds pushed deep down and buried, and no masks to hide the dirties and uglys of life's pain along the way. All they knew was a raw, untainted pure love for each other. Nowadays, there are apps, meet and greets, and those friends arranged hook ups to help find that perfect match. What it comes down to is finding someone who's level of imperfections fits your level of imperfections and the rest is all God. Each and every one of us grow up in varying communities, environments, families and life circumstances that develop our internal, moral compasses that govern right from wrong. What's normal for you, may not be someone else's normal and can look confusing from the outside looking in to their life picture. One of my favorite and most repeated quote is by Alfred Adler; "the only normal people are those you don't know very well." Every counseling session my husband and I have conducted with young couples always come down to one root cause for every issue in their relationship; selfishness. You see, that's what happened to Adam and Eve, Eve let the enemy talk her into questioning God's authority and tempting her with knowledge and power, to be like God, just by eating the forbidden fruit of the tree. (Genesis 3:1-19) It was all about "Self". The divine order of things is to seek God first and He will direct your steps, so if that app leads to who you think is Mr. or Miss Wonderful, run a little prayer by

God and see if you are moving in that right direction. If you are married or in a relationship, remember the importance of placing God first and pray for help in seeking to benefit each other and not just yourself, striving always to fulfill God's will not your own. I Corinthians 13:3-8 contains beautifully detailed instructions on how to love one another. I promise you friends, when you place your trust in God, love never fails.

Wellness

For my birthday last year, a dear friend gifted me a journal. I have been using this journal to record daily, three things I am thankful for. I began my gratitude journal as a challenge with my children. The purpose was to increase our positivity and encourage strong mental health, which is scientifically proven to do so. Gratitude is practiced and by recording and physically writing down three things daily, it will flood your hearts with renewed appreciation for life! When I struggle some mornings, it may be as simple a thing like, "I am breathing" or "I am walking in a new day and alive and well". This simple act reaps such tremendous benefit spiritually, physically and mentally. Among just a few noted benefits are improved self-esteem, better sleep, more joy, reduced stress and more compassion. What are you thankful for today?

Healthy

Wild blueberries are teeny tiny powerhouses of antioxidants, vitamins and minerals. These amazing little wonders are one of the most powerful healing fruits, a gift from God. Domesticated big blueberries are a little different than wild tiny blueberries, as not to confuse the two. Wild blueberries are the same color from the skin to the inside juicy part, containing higher amounts of anthocyanins, which is a polyphenol that can actually cross the blood brain barrier. Wild blueberries are widely studied and clinically proven to be antiviral, antibacterial, anti-inflammatory and improve brain function. They increase memory and aid in the production and restoration of synaptic responses in our brains. They are filled with antioxidants that can potentially detox heavy metals like a magnet, helping to relieve that foggy feeling you may experience throughout the day. With all of the health benefits, it's hard to rationalize not making them a staple in your diet. I use Trader Joe's organic frozen wild blueberries, and include them in my morning shake two to three times a week.

Mirror Message of the Day

I am forgiven, in Christ Jesus. All my sin was cast to the deepest depths of the bottom of the ocean to be no more.
Micah 7:19

Notes

_____

_____

_____

_____

_____

_____

_____

_____

_____

_____

_____

_____

_____

Day 28

"Then God blessed them, and God said to them,
"Be fruitful and multiply; fill the earth and
subdue it; have dominion over the fish of the
sea, over the birds of the air, and over every
living thing that moves on the earth."
Genesis 1:28 ESV

My first horse Shardo was a mustang with a gloriously golden colored coat and creamy mane and tail. I have adored horses from the time I could talk, so my dad waited until the ripe age of seven to gift me my very own. My dad taught me everything I needed to know to care for this towering animal that was literally twenty times my size. Every day I would come home from school, and the pasture was where you would find me. Brushing, exercising, feeding, watering, washing and entertaining full on conversations with him about my day, confiding in him my deepest feelings that a seven year old could possibly have. It must have been a sight to watch me bridle, blanket, saddle, and mount up on this thirteen hand horse by myself, but I did every chance I got without even the slightest hint of fear. I didn't know how to fear him, because I was only taught the authority I held over this majestic animal's behavior, the ability to command him to halt, drop his head, turn left, turn right, walk, gallop and run without faltering or fail. Then came a morning I wanted to go for a ride and my dad said, "We better not today, there are storms moving in". Instead of listening and obeying, I headed out anyway, saddled up and took off up the trail. Once I got to the end of the pasture, it started thundering and the sprinkles of rain began to fall. As I headed back to the stable, lightning struck pretty close and the thunder crashed so loud it spooked Shardo, morphing him instantly to a rearing, bucking bronco! I rode for a few seconds, but the thrush of his hind quarters sent me sailing to the ground. By the grace of God, I stood right up free of any injuries for the exception of a few scratches and one extremely wounded swagger. I learned fear of my horse that day, not frightful fear but reverent fear. You see, the next day, daddy made me get right back up in the saddle to teach me not to be frightful because I still held authority, but be reverent of a horse's strength, size and power. In Deuteronomy 31:12 NKJV, God told Moses to gather the people, men, women and little ones to hear and to LEARN to fear the Lord our God, to teach them by hearing His words. The reverential fear of God must be taught and learned. Amazingly, faith increases and grows right alongside the knowledge of our Father God's great omnipotence, power and glory. His love for us goes beyond measure so acknowledge the omnipresence of God through prayer, praise and worship.

Wellness

As I mentioned before, signs of aging are eminent but as we move through this life we can do our parts to help protect and preserve our bodies and create the least amount of wear and tear we can. I started noticing my first wrinkles on my face when I was around thirty-three. I used to sleep on my stomach and the pressure from laying on my face night after night was forging this deep crease and crevice in my cheek up towards my eye. Logic and physics came in to play. On that day, I decided I was going to train myself to become a back sleeper and I was going to love it! Another anti-wrinkle action I do nightly is massaging my oils into my face in gentle but firm circular motions, concentrating on the area around my lips and between my eyebrows in my furrow, starting on the inside and circling out towards my ears. Just as massage loosens tight muscles in your back, arms and legs, massaging your face will reduce the tension and loosen the cranial muscles in your face. Pick one night per week to spend a little extra time and really give your face some fingertip love!

Healthy

Leafy greens are beautiful, lush and filled with health boosting benefits beyond description! Once you make it a point to add them to your diet daily, it does not take but a few days to literally feel the difference. Spinach, arugula, chard and butter lettuce, are among my favorites, finely chopped and topped with horseradish mustard dressing makes a quick and tasty side to any lunch or dinner. You can even throw in a handful of spinach in your cooked veggie medleys to get them added to your daily diet.

Mirror Message of the Day

I am appointed to be about my Father's business, chosen and set apart.
Luke 2:49

Notes

_____

_____

_____

_____

_____

_____

_____

_____

_____

_____

_____

_____

_____

Day 29

"So God said, "Behold, I have given you every plant yielding seed that is on the face of all the earth, and every tree with seed in its fruit. You shall have them for food."
Genesis 1:29 ESV

Imagine it's your birthday and you have the most beautifully adorned gift presented to you. Carefully, you untie the ribbon, peel back the wrapping paper, and lift out an envelope and in that envelope are ... seeds. Would you be delighted or would you cringe just a little, thinking "what am I supposed to do with these seeds? I think I would be grouped among the later! My initial response is a result of being raised and living with the mindset of instant gratification. Knowing that right now, I can ride on down to the market and buy whatever I need or want already planted, grown, harvested, washed and ready for me to eat. Right now, I wouldn't have to do the work, right now the ground would not have to be prepared, and right now I wouldn't have to trench the seed lines, drop in the seeds, cover the earth on top, water and wait. (Enter Jeopardy theme song) And, we wait some more. And we wait some more, and more. Planting, growing and harvesting requires a lot of time, patience and hard work, and so does just about anything that is worth having. We value the most, what requires the most. One of the most important seeds to plant in relationships is trust, however that trust needs to be rooted in Father God, not in people because every single one of us is fallible. In Jeremiah 17:7-8 ESV the Word says "a man that trusts in the Lord is like a tree planted by the water ... and does not cease to bear fruit". When we root our trust in the Lord, then our confidence and faith grow in each other. Trust that no matter what, the Lord is working all things for our good. (Romans 8:28) Whatever the circumstance may be, we commit it to God in prayer and believe, have faith and trust that it will be, according to His will. Wishy washy believing and going with the ebb and flow of the here and now just won't do. We need to remain steadfast in faith, steadfast in waiting until the seeds we just planted in our prayer start to take root and sprout. You may not see it, but it's coming ... just hold on. Don't be hasty and re-plow the field, killing the seed that you faithfully planted. If you try to plant a different crop now, you will deplete minerals and strength in the soil and the new crop will have its own mess of troubles and difficulty to contend with. Steadfast waiting is always the answer. Stand dutifully firm and unwavering until that day of breakthrough when that sprout pops up and says good morning to the new hope, the wondrous miracle of all God has done!

Wellness

Synthetic chemicals are everywhere and can be difficult to avoid and impossible to eliminate from our day in-day out living. Food packaging, use of microwaves, water bottles, shampoos, lotions, cosmetics, laundry detergents and softeners, even the clothes we wear can leach chemicals on to our skin and be absorbed in our bodies. Xenoestrogens attach to our estrogen receptors and wreak havoc within our endocrine systems by causing estrogen overload. We can limit our exposure by choosing products that are naturally derived and free of the culprit chemical ingredients. I provide a list to avoid in this book, but always encourage you to research for yourselves as well. Granted, we cannot live in a bubble, but that is why good nutrition and eating foods that pull these toxins from our body is vitally important. These are God given tools, so let's use them.

Healthy

Superfoods have gained popularity in the health industry lately and with good reason. The God given tools I spoke about in today's health section is a perfect example of why it's critical for us to incorporate these into our diet daily. The mix I use is organic and contains wheatgrass, barley grass, moringa, spirulina and chlorella. It's so easy to dump a full serving into my morning shake and voila! These powerhouse greens make their way through my body and go right to work, pulling out toxins, heavy metals, boosting immunity and reducing inflammation, which is the number one cause of disease. We may not always control our environment and the toxins we are exposed to daily, but we can help our bodies stay strong and overcome.

Mirror Message of the Day

I am filled with the power of the Holy Spirit and will share all that God has done for me.
Acts 1:8

Notes

Day 30

"AND TO EVERY BEAST OF THE EARTH AND TO EVERY BIRD
OF THE HEAVENS AND TO EVERYTHING THAT CREEPS ON THE
EARTH, EVERYTHING THAT HAS THE BREATH OF LIFE, I HAVE
GIVEN EVERY GREEN PLANT FOR FOOD." AND IT WAS SO.
GENESIS 1:30 ESV

I am a builder of things, that's what I do. I imagine, create a plan, gather the materials and set out to make it all come together as I picture it in my mind's eye. However, if I am lacking the proper tools, making it all come together is a much more difficult task. I love those pieces of furniture that have to be put together and include instructions that start with the "what you will need" list to get the job done. Too many self-assemble projects that ran into the wee hours taught me well to follow that list, and step by step it will come out just like the picture! Life has an instruction book. God wrote it all down and gave it to us so that we would know how to live this life successfully if we just follow the directions. In 2 Timothy 3:16-17 ESV it says "ALL Scripture is breathed out by God and profitable for teaching, for reproof, for correction, and for training in righteousness, that the man of God may be complete, equipped for every good work" and I believe it. I have yet to find a life circumstance not found and talked about in the Word, complete with the solution. Too often, we let our troubles grow so big in our mind's eye, letting them block our vision line of God and become overwhelmed. We speak things like "I don't know what I'm going to do" "It's not fair" "I should just give up" "It's the worst!" "Things will never change!" Well no they won't, not as long as your focus is on your problem and those negative words are spewing out of your mouth. The Word tells us that whatever we speak will be, that our tongue holds the power of life and death, peace or destruction, prosperity or despair, joy or depression, health or sickness, our choice, our words, our responsibility ... Our responses need to be fully considered so they may only encourage, lift up and positively influence others through the love of Christ in us. In order to do this, we will need those proper tools we just talked about. God has granted us all the things that pertain to life (2 Peter 1:3) We do not have to succumb to the hurts this world dishes out, we are Jesus' righteousness and heir to the throne of the one true King of kings, Lord of lords. I abide in Him and He is faithful to shelter me in the storms of life. We defeat the enemy the same way Jesus did, by audibly speaking forth the promises of God from His Word. Dress up in that full armor of God He has given us. Fasten the belt of truth, put on that breastplate of righteousness, shoes on your feet and take up that shield of faith. Place the helmet of salvation on your head and pick up your sword of the Spirit. All of these are the most valued tools for success. (Ephesians 6:13-17) Get going, fully dressed my darling, and shine your brightest today!

Wellness

Sometimes we grow weary in our health and physical endeavors, we get tired and just want to be still and lay down the heaviness of those weights and that's okay! As I said before, even Jesus grew tired and needed to rest. The key is not remaining there, but rise up, look up, keep your eyes physically, mentally and spiritually fixed on God because this is our source of renewed strength. He is our only source for the rest and stillness we need. Sit down in the comfort seat, fix your eyes on Jesus this morning. Cast those cares, release control and start this day in the assurance of His mercy, grace and great unmerited favor that is lavished upon you. This is His gift to you through His righteousness.

Healthy

Remember, our bodies are quite literally what we eat, drink, smell and lather on our skin. Everything we come in contact with surges through our blood, infused and used by each cell that makes us, well … us. My first meal of the day is a shake, or smoothie because food is medicine and I believe this one discipline has improved my health exponentially. Regardless if you are a breakfast eater or skipper, consider this quick and easy nutritional boost to start your day out right. There are special occasions that call for an actual breakfast, and then I just trade the time of my shake with another meal. The benefits of combining everything in a tasty shake is by blending, your food is so much easier to digest and becomes more bioavailable. Your system will not have to work so hard breaking everything down before absorption. I am able to get a caloric boost, because basically I was walking around in starvation mode for years, prior. Loading those good quality calories, I stay full longer and do not eat as much the rest of the day, keeping my binging moments at a minimum. With all the organic frozen fruits and veggies, the time it takes to prepare a shake is about ten to fifteen minutes, tops. Now that I have talked you into trying, please explore some of my favorite creations found in the recipes section.

Mirror Message of the Day

I have true life because God's Spirit lives in me and my spirit is alive! Romans 8:11

Notes

_____

_____

_____

_____

_____

_____

_____

_____

_____

_____

_____

_____

Whew! Thirty days! You made it! I pray you have established new protocols in your life routine, adjusted priorities, valuing YOU. Continue your healing journey through going back over these pages and re-reading your notes. Consider the health portions and where they may easily fit with your lifestyle, creating permanent changes and will benefit you the most. You may even start over for another thirty days for God has a way, through the divine awesomeness of the Holy Spirit, to open our eyes to something different each time. He is faithful to reveal what needs to be done to walk a successful and fulfilling life He designed just for you. The Word says the wisdom is there for the asking so that is all you have to do, just ask.

"Holy Spirit lead me, direct me and guide me in Your wisdom today. Give me Your Words to build others up today, keep my hands from evil so I may not cause any pain. Bless me and keep me in Your unmerited favor and number my steps for Your glory. You, Father are so good and Your mercy endures forever! In Jesus' name, Amen."

Shake it Up
Recipes

Pineapple Upside Down Shake

½ cup frozen organic pineapple
1 whole organic banana, peeled
½ red organic apple with peel
4-5 whole medjool dates
¼ cup shelled pecans
½ cup organic coconut milk
½ cup water
2 tbsp ground organic flax seed
1 tbsp. organic chia seed
1 tsp Yoursuper organic super greens
½ tsp ceylon cinnamon
½ ground organic ginger
Pinch of ground organic clove
⅛ tsp ground milk thistle
1 Tbsp MCT oil
1 Tbsp hydrolyzed collagen protein
1 Tbsp Yoursuper vegan protein
Blend and enjoy!

Lori's Go to Morning Detox Shake

1 cup frozen organic strawberries
1 whole organic banana, peeled
½ cup organic wild blueberries
4-5 pitted dark cherries
½ cup organic coconut milk
½ cup water
2 tbsp. ground organic flax seed
1 tbsp. organic chia seed
1 tsp Yoursuper organic super greens
1 tsp Yoursuper Your beautiful blend
½ tsp ceylon cinnamon
⅛ tsp ground milk thistle
1 Tbsp. MCT oil
1 Tbsp. hydrolyzed collagen protein
1 Tbsp. Yoursuper vegan protein
Blend and Enjoy!

Carrot Cake Shake

1 whole banana, peeled
2 organic medium sized carrots, peeled and sliced
½ organic red apple with peel
½ cup organic raisins
¼ cup shelled pecans
½ cup organic coconut milk
½ cup water
2 tbsp. ground organic flax seed
1 tbsp. organic chia seed
1 tsp Yoursuper organic super greens
½ tsp ground organic ginger
Pinch of ground organic clove
½ tsp ceylon cinnamon
⅛ tsp ground milk thistle
1 Tbsp. MCT oil
1 Tbsp. hydrolyzed collagen protein
1 Tbsp. Yoursuper vegan protein
Blend and Enjoy!

Raspberry Muffin Shake

1 whole organic banana
1 Cup organic frozen raspberries
½ organic red apple with peel
¼ cup of shelled pecans
4-5 whole medjool dates
½ cup organic coconut milk
½ cup water
2 tbsp. ground organic flax seed
1 tbsp. organic chia seed
1 tsp Yoursuper organic super greens
1 tsp Yoursuper Your beautiful blend
½ tsp ceylon cinnamon
⅛ tsp ground milk thistle
1 Tbsp. MCT oil
1 Tbsp. hydrolyzed collagen protein
1 Tbsp. Yoursuper vegan protein
Blend and Enjoy!

Fig newton cookie shake

1 whole frozen organic banana
½ organic red apple with peel
4-5 whole dried organic figs
¼ cup shelled pecans
½ cup organic coconut milk
½ cup water
2 tbsp. ground organic flax seed
1 tbsp. organic chia seed
1 tsp Yoursuper organic super greens
½ tsp organic ground ginger
Pinch of organic ground clove
½ tsp ceylon cinnamon
⅛ tsp ground milk thistle
1 Tbsp. MCT oil
1 Tbsp. hydrolyzed collagen protein
1 Tbsp. Yoursuper vegan protein
Blend and Enjoy!

Blueberry Muffin Shake

1 whole organic banana
½ cup organic wild blueberries
½ cup organic blueberries
½ peeled organic red apple
½ cup organic coconut milk
½ cup water
2 tbsp. ground organic flax seed
1 tbsp. organic chia seed
1 tsp Yoursuper organic super greens
1 tsp Yoursuper Your beautiful blend
½ tsp ceylon cinnamon
⅛ tsp ground milk thistle
1 Tbsp. MCT oil
1 Tbsp. hydrolyzed collagen protein
1 Tbsp. Yoursuper vegan protein
Blend and Enjoy!

All things Pumpkin Shake

1 whole frozen organic banana
1 Cup organic canned pumpkin (bpa free can)
½ frozen organic red apple peeled
4 whole organic dried dates
½ cup organic coconut milk
½ cup water
2 tbsp. ground organic flax seed
1 tbsp. organic chia seed
1 tsp Yoursuper organic super greens
½ tsp ceylon cinnamon
½ tsp organic ground ginger
Pinch of organic ground clove
⅛ tsp ground milk thistle
1 Tbsp. MCT oil
1 Tbsp. hydrolyzed collagen protein
1 Tbsp. Yoursuper vegan protein
Blend and Enjoy!

Choosing organic foods is that important because of the enormous amount of chemicals and genetic manipulation that is happening within our world's produce. Organic certification is saying the seeds or plants to grow this produce you just bought have not been genetically altered or treated with pesticides, and herbicides. The Environmental Working Group or EWG has compiled a list based on third party testing to determine the top twelve highest contaminated produce and deemed should always be purchased organic. They also released the top fifteen cleanest produce items that don't always need to be organic, but please, always wash them thoroughly. You never know what has come into contact in transport or the back room of the distributor or store.

Dirty Twelve

1. Strawberries
2. Spinach
3. Kale
4. Nectarines
5. Apples
6. Grapes
7. Peaches
8. Cherries
9. Pears
10. Tomatoes
11. Celery
12. Potatoes

Clean Fifteen

1. Avocados
2. Sweet Corn
3. Pineapple
4. Onions
5. Papaya
6. Sweet Peas (frozen)
7. Eggplant

8. Asparagus
9. Cauliflower
10. Cantaloupe
11. Broccoli
12. Mushrooms
13. Cabbage
14. Honeydew Melon
15. Kiwi

Special acknowledgement to Shane Ellison, author of *Over the Counter Natural Cures*.

This is the Dirty Dozen list I reference in my text. Always check your ingredients of food, supplements, sports powders, drinks, etc. I strongly recommend avoiding products containing any of the additives below.

- Titanium Dioxide
- Magnesium Stearate
- Carrageenan
- Silicon Dioxide
- Calcium Carbonate
- Glucose Syrup
- Sucrose
- Dextrose
- High Fructose Corn Syrup
- Chromium
- Cholecalciferol (synthetic vitamin D)